i

Visit Mike at his web site

www.mikeschaffer.com

For more books, videos, and information about
Lessons, clinics and training.

Riding in the Moment

Discover the Hidden Language of Dressage

By
Michael Schaffer

ISBN:1460932641
Library of Congress Control Number: 2011902871

Table of Contents

Section I - Hiding in Plain Sight

Section II - Developing the Basics

Section III - Working with the Basics

Acknowledgments

First on the list has to be Kathy Von Ertfelda. Although she's been helpful in ways big and small for decades, a few years ago she invited me up to her farm, provided me with a demo horse, and spent a couple of days taking most of the pictures in this book. It's hard to imagine how this project could have taken form without her efforts and generosity. Another major supporter in this work is Debra Strong. She's been reading and commenting on most of these chapters — many several times over as I've written, rewritten, and rewritten again. Michelle Doty also lent a big hand in finding the kind of small mistakes that just don't want to go away. A special note of thanks goes to KW who helped more than she knows, and to TR who shot the pictures in the chapter on Ground work.

Section 1
The Hidden Language
of Dressage

1 Hiding in Plain Sight

*T*he dressage lexicon, the written and spoken words of dressage, is suitable for teaching a student how to ride a dressage horse, but inadequate and problematic for teaching a student or reader how to train one.

The first problem with the language is that it's top down. It begins at its end point with definitions and descriptions of trained horses ridden with refined aids. Even the most basic exercises are defined in their finished form — circles are round, serpentine loops are even, and transitions are done on the mark.

The language does do a good job of defining the perfect form of each exercise and the ideal qualities we seek in all of them. It also provides the general order for introducing the movements and figures. However, it doesn't explain how the figures and movements are trained, it only tells us how to ride them — and it tells us that with misleading mechanical words!

Dressage phrases like "bend the horse around your inside leg" and "push him up to the bit" literally tell us to "bend" our horses and "push" them to the bit by physically pushing, pulling, and bending. Without interpretation these statements are terribly confusing.

Humans are not physically capable of bending a horse or pushing him anyplace he doesn't want to go to. This is why trainers go through a cognitive process of teaching the horse to bend, to step up to the bit, and to move from the leg. Then, when the horse understands these ideas and the aids for them, it will feel to the rider as though he bent the horse and pushed him to the bit.

So, the dressage lexicon tells us "what" to train not "how" to train. Worse, it doesn't even have the words to explain training. The language is top down and mechanical, but training a dressage horse is a bottom up, cognitive process. This is why even the most basic levels of dressage have been so frustrating to so many for so long. Without words and concepts, learning has been totally dependant on the experience and feel that comes from access to advanced horses and instructors. I was very lucky to have had some opportunities to ride a few school masters in my early dressage education.

I'll never forget my first ride on a wonderful old Grand Prix horse. He was totally different from anything I had felt to that point. He used his back, bent, and reached out softly to the bit. A few minutes into the ride I was asked to do a half-pass. I had never done one before, but I knew what they were supposed to look like and what the aids should be, so I tried it. Amazing! He did this wonderful half-pass. Then, he did it in the other direction just as easily and just as well.

I had many firsts on him that day, my first few steps of piaffe and passage, my first real extended trot — it was quite a lesson. The flying changes stood out especially. When asked to do one on the diagonal, I pointed him across the ring and at the halfway point moved my new outside leg back. That easily I had just done my first flying change. Cool. Of course we had to do one the other way — no problem. Then I was asked to do changes, four strides apart on the next diagonal. Smooth as silk. My gosh, I had gone from a training level to a fourth level rider in just a few minutes! It got better, I was then told to do a diagonal of changes every three strides, followed by a diagonal of changes every two strides. After that, I was asked to just stay on the rail.

I was cantering up the long side trying to digest the last few minutes of flying changes when I heard the instructor say, "Don't let him do that!" I wasn't quite sure what she meant, but something did feel a bit strange, so I leaned forward and peeked over his shoulder. He was doing changes every stride — one tempis! It actually took another trip around the arena to teach me how to make him stop doing those and just canter again.

...it didn't give me the tools, or even the words, to deal with a green or badly trained horse.

Aside from all of these firsts, this ride set my standards for what a correct horse should feel like. I still think of him when a horse I'm working with becomes soft, springy, and effortless to ride. It also had a tremendous effect on my thinking about dressage — but that didn't begin until two days later.

I couldn't wait to get home and try what I had learned in those lessons on my off the track thoroughbred. I had last been on him several days before, when I was at best a marginal training level rider. Now, I had ridden almost all the Grand Prix movements. Something had to have changed in me that would have a dramatic affect on him!

It didn't. He was exactly the same. His back was stiff, his stride choppy, his mouth hard and unyielding. The only change was that I knew how stiff, choppy, and unyielding he was. What was the matter? Why couldn't I ride my own horse the way I rode the school master just a few days before?

The answer is obvious — he wasn't trained and I wasn't equipped to solve training problems. The dressage education I had to that point, like the language of dressage, was top down. It had developed my eye enough that I could watch a Grand Prix test and come up with about the same score as an international judge. It taught me enough about the aids and developed my seat to the point that I could ride a finished horse. But it didn't give me the tools, or even the words, to deal with a green or badly trained horse.

...something did feel a bit strange, so I leaned forward and peeked over his shoulder.

To show you how limited the words of dressage are for dealing with basic problems, I'll jump forward a good number of years to a clinic I was teaching. One lesson started off with the horse stiff and pulling so I asked the rider to stop. I got no reaction so I asked again, but the horse and rider continued. So, I waited. Finally, a circle or two later, the student stopped.

"What's the problem?" I asked. "Stopping isn't a big deal, just make the horse stop. "

"I was trying to prepare him," came the reply.

Well, as soon as it was said, I realized that this student, sitting in a dressage saddle, riding in a dressage ring, in front of a dressage instructor, was in the same spot I was in on my stiff off the track thoroughbred. She had no word for stop in her language — dressage speak. The closest translation available is "halt", and halt is not something to be entered into rashly. It requires careful consideration, thoughtful reflection, and much making ready.

Ok, I'm having a little fun with this, but that student was in a very real predicament.   Said in dressage speak, the horse was:

"Resisting"
or "evasive"
or "against the aids"
or "behind the aids"
or "running through the aids"
and she was trying to use the "aids"
to "half-halt"
in preparation for a "transition"
to a "halt".

That half-halts, transitions, and halts all require the horse to be very much "on the aids" is the Catch-22 that so many riders find many riders find themselves in.

It's easy to see the problem in this example, but riders who try to hold their horses "on the aids" and in a frame with strong hands, or make them "forward" with tight legs and spurs are making the same mistake. They are all trying to get their horses to learn about dressage the way they did — in a human, top down fashion. They think if they can make their horses do what they're supposed to, by using whatever force they have to, their horses will understand what they want.   They hope this will develop the qualities of a good dressage horse.

But it never works that way — not ever. Horses don't start with a concept of a half-pass and then try to figure out how to do it. That's top down learning. Training horses is a bottom up process. A trainer has to start with something that's easy for the horse to do and a little like a half-pass. As the horse begins to understand this early exercise, the trainer increases his demands — always keeping it easy for the horse. Over time the horse will understand a finished "half-pass" as a concept. When he does, he'll perform them just as easily as that wonderful old schoolmaster did for me so long ago.

The cognitive, bottom up process of training a dressage horse begins with what I'm calling "first tier basics". They are: go, stop, turn in, move out, and soften. Although these concepts are hidden deep within the language, they are at the core of everything in dressage. We build from these to create all of the figures, movements, and qualities we want in our horses.

These basics are comprehensible, attainable, and immediate. You don't have to experience them on advanced school masters, you can achieve each of these on your horse today or in the next several days. As you do, your horse will begin to understand the first tier basics and become responsive to your "aids" for them. Then, you will be able to make progress — until then, you won't. Either you'll be stuck at the lowest levels trying to ride round circles forever, or you'll end up forcing horses to perform in a way that makes them stiff, sore, and ultimately lame. It is this black and white, this straight forward, this simple.

Exploring these concepts and showing you how to use them to train a dressage horse will take the rest of this book. However, before you can understand the process, you need a bottom up understanding of dressage.

2 A Few Simple Words

*F*OR ALL THE millions of words written about dressage and all the billions spoken, we literally don't know what we're talking about.   This is because "dressage" does not have a definition — a concise explanation of its meaning.

To be certain the word has a translation: it comes from the French word for "training." However, dressage is only one form of training, and the translation does nothing to explain what separates it from other programs.   This makes the origin of the word an interesting, but absolutely useless, bit of trivia.

Many might look to FEI Article 401 for clarification, but that goes on for a total of 496 words which is hardly concise.   In addition, the language used is technical and many of those words require their own long interpretations.

Explaining dressage in general terms doesn't work either.   Saying it's "systematic" or results in "harmony" between horse and rider, ignores the fact that all good training is systematic and results in harmony between trainer and trainee.   These statements are only true of dressage — not unique to it.   The phrase "ballet on horseback" could be applicable to any well-ridden horse in any discipline, and, to be frank, the modern dressage horse reminds me more of Astaire's grace than Baryshnikov's leaps.

It means we don't have to make our horses perform, we have to show them they're allowed to perform.

The real problem with these attempts to explain, describe, or compare dressage is that they all allude to its advanced form. They all talk about what is supposed to happen at some time in the future, after you've done dressage for long enough. Even our non-verbal image is advanced — say the word and you picture a rider in shadbelly and top hat on a collected horse.   But dressage is more than a clever rider on an advanced horse doing fancy tricks — it's about the process that got them there.   For us to really "know" what we're talking about, we need a few simple words that will explain what it means for you to be doing dressage today — alone, on your horse, in your schooling area.

There are a few words and they are simple —

dressage: a method of teaching horses the most efficient and comfortable way to carry riders.

That's it. Dressage teaches a horse that the easiest, most comfortable way to carry his rider is by bending and stepping out to corners. This encourages him to stretch over his top line to the bit and engage his hind legs. A horse engages when he bends the three joints of his hind legs equally as he brings them under his body. Engaging allows him to use the power of the hind legs to lift which, along with stretching to the bit, makes the horse round and raise his back. This method of lifting a rider is the equine equivalent of humans learning to pick up heavy objects by bending at the knees and lifting with their legs, instead of bending at the waist and straining their back.

The idea that dressage teaches horses the easiest most comfortable way to carry riders should shape everything we do. It means we don't have to make our horses perform, we have to show them they're allowed to perform. This is the most important idea in dressage. It should be the crucible through which all of our thoughts, every method and technique we use must pass.

3 The Big Easy

*O*NE OF LIFE'S most beautiful symmetries is that things get easier as you learn the best way to do them. It makes no difference what it is — a chore at work, changing a tire, making dinner, mucking a stall, or training a horse — the better you get at doing something, the easier it is do.

Everything in our experience supports this. Nobody ever looks for a harder more frustrating way to do something. No one has ever rushed into his boss's office proclaiming, "I should get a raise, I just figured out a much harder way to do my job!" Ease is such a high priority it is among the first qualities reviewed when analyzing any new method. If you begin to do something a new way and see it's making things more difficult, you abandon that approach and look for another.

Easy does not mean without effort, or doing it the 'easy' way instead of doing it right. Easy means you're doing the best job possible, with the least amount of effort, and doing it without physical or mental stress. By this standard, ease is tantamount to correct. It's an important and highly reliable guide to training methods. If you and your horse find dressage challenging, but are relaxed and enjoying yourselves, you're probably doing it right. On the other hand, if you're finding things really difficult, or you're frustrated

and not progressing, you need to look for an easier way to ride —
not a harder way.

Yet the chances are high the instructors you go to are in the business
because riding came easily to them. The problem with this is that
very often people who naturally find something easy, don't
comprehend why it doesn't come just as easily to everybody else.
Furthermore, because it has come naturally to them, they rarely know
precisely what it is that they're actually doing and why it seems
effortless. But although they find it easy, in an all too human trait,
they are often the first to tell everybody else the way to succeed is
to work much harder at it.

However, there are perils in trying to work "harder" at dressage. The
first is that you can't work harder without making your horse work
harder. Working your horse too hard makes him defensive — he
begins to worry that he can't figure out what you want, or that he
won't have enough energy to keep going for an entire schooling
session. When this happens, he'll stop trying to perform and begin
trying to avoid performing.

Another problem with the idea of working harder is that many people
interpret it to mean they should use their "aids" with more physical
effort. This creates stiffness and tension in you that goes directly
to the horse and makes him stiff and tense. Whatever quality of
dressage you were seeking by working harder is now further from
you, not closer. Dressage is an art — the skill of this art is in getting
the horse to perform happily, without stress or tension in you or the
horse.

How easy is easy? The answer is really quite straightforward. Riding
a well trained horse of any discipline should be easier than walking.
How much effort does it take for you to go, stop, or turn when you
are walking? That is more effort than it should take to do the same
on a horse.

Trying to do dressage easily is not a radical idea. The two most important exercises of classical dressage rely on the fact that it is easier for the horse to perform correctly than incorrectly — although, it's not often explained this way.

The first exercise is based on the fact that it is easier for a horse to *soften*, bend, and *move out* to a circle large enough that he can be comfortable, than to fall in to a small circle out of balance and out of rhythm.

the same thing said in dressage speak is, "do a volte."

So, whenever a horse goes above the bit, or loses bend, the rider simply has to either allow the horse to fall in or lead him to a small circle. With some correct basic training a horse will soon realize the difficulty he's in and try to eliminate it by bending correctly and moving out to a larger circle. The approach of using small circles to fix problems should not sound new — the same thing said in dressage speak is "do a volte." This idea of using a circle small enough that the horse self-corrects is a central theme in training that I return to over and over again.

The second technique is based on the fact that, within reasonable limits, it's easier for a horse to just keep going than to keep stopping and going. The logic of this is clear when you think of pushing a car. It is far easier to get it going and keep it going than to keep stopping it and then starting it rolling again. Like a car, a horse is big enough that overcoming inertia by having to stop and start again is a noticeable strain in comparison to just continuing on.

So one of the most important (and underutilized) training techniques we have is to simply stop the horse when he does not respond as requested. By stopping the horse every time he fails to respond to you, he'll soon learn it's far easier to just pay attention to your aids than not. This too has its classical counterpart — said in dressage speak it becomes, "do a transition."

This brings us back to the starting point of that poor student trying to "do a transition" on a horse that is not on the aids. However, before we're ready to deal with that, we need to clear up a few more concepts about riding.

4 Tools of the Trade

*I*n order to train horses, you must be able to use your hands, seat, and legs in three distinct ways: "connected", "cognitive" and "mechanical".   The idea that we have three separate, well defined ways to use our aids stands in stark contrast to the conventional language of dressage that only describes the aids in the ideal, finished form.

Just having the concept of ideal aids makes no accommodation for the infinite set of circumstances and challenges that commonly occur in training.   So the aspiring rider and his instructor have no words, and therefore no concepts, to explain how they are dealt with.

The adage, "When your only tool is a hammer, every problem looks like a nail," applies here.   In this context the ideal aids are the hammer and the solution to every problem is to exaggerate them by using "more inside leg", "more outside hand", more this, or more that.

Successful trainers don't limit themselves to ideal aids. Although they don't explain it very well, careful observation will show that they do use cognitive, connected, and mechanical versions of aids on a regular basis to deal with the everyday details of horse training.

Briefly stated, "cognitive" use of hand, seat and legs relies solely on the horse's understanding of its meaning for its effectiveness. Cognitive aids "signal" or "cue" the horse what is wanted, but in no way compel performance.   "Connected" aids are the ideal traditionally defined aids used for dressage. While connected aids should be as subtle as those used on the best cognitively trained horses, these also rely on the horse moving freely forward into an accepting hand with his back up and quarters engaged. "Mechanical" methods are used to physically control the horse. In terms of developing the dressage horse, cognitive and mechanical methods are only applicable when training the first tier basics. All other figures and movements must be done with a connected horse reaching forward into ideal aids.

Mechanical

Mechanical aids or techniques may be properly used as "corrections" to physically stop a horse from doing what is wrong or to show him what is right. Mechanical methods are only properly used in training the five first tier basics and only for a few moments at a time.

Momentary mechanical techniques degenerate into mechanical, backwards riding when they are used as "aids" to ride the horse instead of tools to assist in training for a few seconds at a time.   I refer to riders that constantly use mechanical aids as "mechanical riders." Rather than trying to make the horse understand what they want, mechanical riders are always trying to make him do what they want. A mechanical rider is always pulling the horse around, using strong legs or kicks. There is no appeal to the horse's intellect and precious little and very ineffective attempts to teach the horse what is correct.

In most disciplines, riding mechanically is just ugly and harsh. Although the rider uses strong hands and legs, at least they let go when they've made whatever point they had in mind. In dressage, mechanical riding is worse because the riders never let go. They use the reins to hold the horse's head in a forced frame while trying to send him forward. This leaves them always jamming on the brakes and gas, ultimately making the horse stiff, sour, and sore.

To make matters more confusing, some horses (usually the large warmbloods) tolerate strong mechanical riding for long enough that they are able to do some advanced movements — they just aren't that good. A horse stamping his feet angrily at the ground in what is supposed to be a piaffe is an example of high level, low quality, mechanical riding. A horse that shortens his stride and flails his tail during flying changes is indicative of mechanical riding. So, it is possible to make horses perform mechanically, but why bother?

Mechanically ridden horses never become submissive or calm. Rather than accepting the rider as the leader who will guide them safely through a worrisome world, they see the rider as just one more worrisome thing in the world.

Cognitive Riding

Virtually the opposite of mechanical riding, cognitive riding has no mechanical effect and relies totally on the horse's intellect. It requires the horse to learn the concepts and tasks necessary for the performance of his job, and the meanings of the various aids the rider uses. It is the most important approach to training there is regardless of discipline.

Trainers who are concerned with making the horse understand the concept of what is wanted, rather than with just making horses do what is wanted, are by my definition, "cognitive trainers. " Cognitive training is valid for all forms of horse related activities and there are some excellent horsemen in many different disciplines doing it. Their techniques vary but their method is the same — they keep chipping away at a concept they want the horse to understand by making tiny little advances followed with immediate, frequent reward. This approach to helping the horse understand what is wanted is the reason a cognitive trainer always keeps his horse calm, relaxed, and happy.

The understanding that comes from cognitive training also creates submission. Riding is herding the horse from the saddle, so as the horse learns what is expected and does it, he is submitting to the leader of the herd of two. As in all herds he learns to look to the leader for safety and security. The more submissive he becomes the more relaxed and calm he gets.

Over time, cognitively trained horses figure out the underlying ideas of the immediate, single tasks their riders have been asking for. Then, they start to put them together into more advanced concepts. As they do, they learn their jobs and become trained. They become the patient old school masters that reward new students with correct movements for correct riding. They are the handy jumpers that safely dig their riders out of horrendously bad spots, and the wise old trail horses that quietly take their hopelessly lost navigators home at the end of the day. All good citizens of the equine world.

Since cognitive riding depends on the horse's understanding, the aids, cues, or signals the rider uses are light. When a horse knows a light touch of legs means go, there is no need to squeeze or kick. If the horse knows he should stop when the rider sits up and touches the reins gently, there is no need to pull. When using cognitive aids no attempt is made to put the horse in a frame, to bend, or collect him. If there is contact it must be feather light and non-restrictive. Once the horse knows what is expected and does it easily, correct contact will develop as the horse becomes connected.

Big Cognitive

There's a special case of cognitive aids that I call "Big Cognitive." These are still light touches or vibrations of the rein, but they're done from an exaggerated position. For instance a leading or opening rein done in a very obvious but still light way would be a big cognitive aid. It's cognitive because it's not mechanically turning or pulling the horse, but it's big because you may have opened your rein a considerable amount. This would be like asking the horse to turn to the right by opening the right rein so much you're pointing to the right but not pulling the horse to the right.

Connected Riding

Connected riding is the gateway and dividing line between riding in general and dressage. Said in dressage speak a "connected" horse is "on the bit" or "on the aids" and is reaching out to the rider's hand, engaging his hind quarters and raising his back. The word "connected" is often used to describe this way of moving because the horse is literally connected from back to front and moves as a whole — all the different parts are working together giving the impression of effortless, often weightless, movement.

Another reason for describing this as connected is that the rider does get a very real sensation of being a part of the horse — you can feel the energy coming from the horse's quarters through his back, into your hand, and then through your back into the horse.

.. a connected horse is "on the bit" or "on the aids'...

"Connection" must come from the horse. Many may find it hard to believe that a horse will voluntarily bend, stretch, and reach out to the bridle, but riding the horse out to his frame is a keystone of forward riding.

However, before a horse can become connected he must be light to the aids, calm, and relaxed. These are qualities that can only be developed by cognitive riding. He must be light to the hand because you can't send your horse out to the bit if he's already pulling on it. He must be light to the leg because he won't learn to bend and stretch his body if you're poking him with a spur or hitting him with a whip. He must be calm and relaxed mentally because he won't be able to relax physically if he is not.

It is common to confuse a connected horse reaching forward to the bit and moving easily from the leg with the pulling and squeezing of forced mechanical riding. In large part this confusion comes from the use of mechanical words to describe ideal aids. "Push your horse from inside leg to outside hand," "bend your horse around your inside leg," and "push your horse up to the bit," are all mechanical descriptions of how it feels to ride a well trained horse. The key phrase in this is "well trained horse. " If your horse already knows to soften and go into the hand correctly, than it will feel as though you "pushed him up to the bit," when in reality you just asked him to do it. If your horse already knows to bend as he moves out, than it will feel exactly like you "bent him around your inside leg" as he moved out. The important thing is, if your horse is properly trained, you're not pushing and bending and moving. You're asking with light easy aids and your horse is willingly and happily responding.

If you're not sure if your horse is properly connected or if you've fallen into the trap of mechanical riding, there are some questions or tests you can use as a guide for yourself.

The first is to ask yourself, "can I choose to ride my horse cognitively — on feather light aids with little or no contact?" If the answer is no, than you cannot be riding in a properly connected way. Another test is to put your horse on a circle, then drop the contact on the inside. If the horse runs off the circle, loses his bend, or changes his stride and tempo, you were holding him back mechanically with the inside rein rather than riding him forward to the connection of the outside rein. Yet another test is to ride your horse on contact, and then drop it. If you just drop the aids — let go of the reins, sit down and do nothing and your horse just stops, that is a pretty good indication that you were riding correctly. However, if you drop the rein and your horse sticks his head up and goes trotting or cantering off, you were absolutely riding mechanically and holding him in a frame with your hands.

Exercise Reward Cycle - Refined!

To understand the roles of these three ways of riding, and how they apply to training the first tier basics, it is necessary to revisit the concepts of the Exercise Reward Cycle that I introduced in *"Right From the Start — Create a Sane, Soft, Well-Balanced Horse."*

The concepts of connected, cognitive, and mechanical riding merge with the exercise reward cycle as it applies to the first tier basics by restating it as,

"First ask correctly with a "cognitive" aid that requests, encourages and allows.

Then, if necessary, make the horse correct in a way that may be "mechanical" but must be clear, effective and over with.

Finally, reward immediately and proportionally."

"Connected" riding results from using the exercise reward cycle. When repeating an exercise, you will know that the horse is starting to understand when he begins to reach out into the hand and seeks contact or connection with the rider through the rein. So, when training first tier basics you ask with cognitive aids, and may have to use mechanical corrections. When working on anything else, you want your horse connected or "on the bit. " If he performs well, you still reward proportionately and immediately. However, if you're having any problem, it will always trace back to one or more first tier basics and so you need to figure out which one and work on that beginning with cognitive aids.

5 A Single Idea

*T*o be an effective trainer, you must reduce any concepts, thoughts, and goals you want to convey to your horse into single ideas. It's essential that you put your training into single ideas because your only way of communicating them to your horse is by converting them to single tasks. So when training, any idea you want to get across to your horse must meet the following criteria:

• First, it must be clear to you. If what you want is not absolutely clear to you, it is absolutely impossible for you to make it clear to the horse.

• Second, it must be precise, specific, and narrow so that you can reduce it to a single task or action that you want you horse to do.

• Third, it must be immediate — present tense. What do you want your horse to do right now — in this moment? Whatever you're asking must be for this stride or the next few, but not beyond.

... he was not taught these movements and concepts in complex form he was taught simple easy ideas...

A single idea converted to a single action is the limit of what we can convey to a horse. I don't know if that's our limit to communicate or the horse's limit to assimilate, but I do know it's the limit. I also know that if I use single, precise, present tense tasks with my horses, they will very shortly begin to generalize the idea. Soon, they seem able to put simple ideas together into more advanced concepts. Then, they start to anticipate and put them in short term future tense. They learn the movements, they learn what's expected of them, they become trained. Speak to them in a way they can accept, and they learn — they understand.

How much do they accept, learn and understand? In the first chapter I told you of my experience on a school master who knew the movements so well that even a beginner like I was got credible results just by "pressing the buttons." He understood that if he had just done 3 tempi and 2 tempi changes he should do 1tempi changes next. However, he was not taught these movements and concepts in complex form — he was taught simple easy ideas that were put together over time until he finally understood the more complex finished movements.

The best trainers are very good at breaking the complex into simple single ideas and tasks. However, the conventional language of dressage is not — it deals with medium and long term goals: entire figures, movements, tests, and levels. But to succeed at any kind of training, you must learn to break your long and medium term goals into simple, single, present tense tasks.

It took me a long time to learn to think in single ideas and tasks. I like to think of entire topics in enough range and detail to fill books. I like to use long explanations to support my reasoning and put my arguments in proper context. Horses definitely "get" context — that's how they decode our aids in fairly complex ways. But horses most certainly do not get long explanations — they get simple, short, precise singular tasks and ideas.

Go, stop, turn in, move out and *soften* are simple, single ideas.

"Impulsion" and "forward" are not single ideas, they are very complex concepts.

Bend and straightness are not single ideas — they are the result of many ideas being used to help the horse learn how to balance under a rider.

Figures and movements, no matter how simple they may seem at first, are not single ideas. Just as there is no single aid for a 20 meter circle, there is no single idea for riding a 20 meter circle.

The way to ride 20 meter circles and every other figure and movement using single present-tense ideas is to literally ride them one stride at a time. For each stride we emphasize the basic we need to keep our horses movement in balance, and create the figure and quality we want.

When riding on a circle, we ask him to *move out* to it with our *move out* aids. Then we prevent him from moving out too much and falling off the circle with our *turn in* aids. We balance his speed, stride and frame with our *go, stop, and soften* aids.

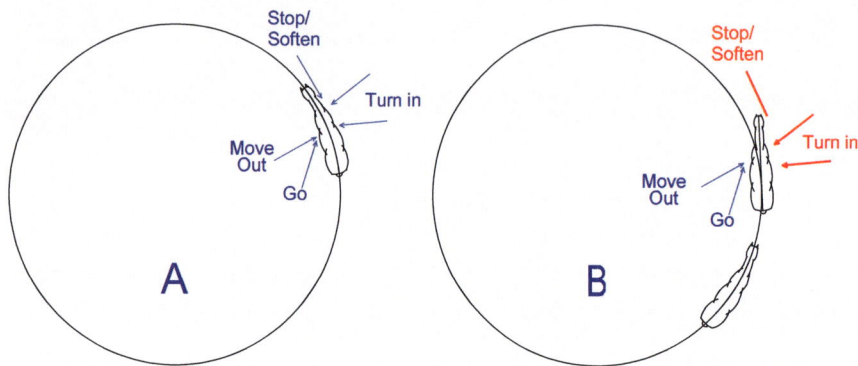

Figure 5-1

The horse on circle -A- shows all the basics working correctly. The horse on circle -B- is not responsive to the *stop* and *turn in* aids, so he is running off the circle.

In the conventional explanation of the aids, we keep a horse on the circle by "pushing him from our inside leg to our outside hand and leg", or "keeping him between our leg and hand." These are mechanical descriptions that lead to mechanical thinking and corrections. The typical mechanical "fix" when a horse runs off the circle is to tell the student to use "more" outside hand or leg. The problem with this is that by the time the student is using enough outside hand or leg, he is using so much it's impossible to ride in a relaxed soft way. So, rather than the rider teaching the horse to go correctly, the horse has taught the rider to ride badly.

To avoid this and many other problems, think of a horse "on the aids" as being so responsive to your aids for the five first tier basics that you can ride in a loose relaxed way. When a horse is on these first tier aids, you ask for each one as necessary to create the movement, figure, or quality you want. In this way, each basic is balanced by another — *go* is balanced with *stop*. *Move out* is not an uncontrolled falling out because it is balanced with *turn in*. Using this approach we change the movement by changing the balance of the aids.

When the basics are out of balance, for instance when a horse is running off the circle, we don't use more aids. We identify which of the basics the horse is not responding to and just work on that until the horse becomes responsive to our best correct aids. In the example above, since the horse is not turning in easily, we abandon the circle for a few minutes and work only on the *turn in* basic with turning in exercises until the horse responds correctly to our light correct aids.

In the next section of this book I'll give you some exercises and ideas for putting your horse on the aids for each of the five first tier basics. After that, I spend a little time explaining how to use the five basics to start riding figures and movements so you can progress up the ranks of dressage.

As your horse becomes more advanced you'll begin to concentrate more and more on the subtleties of advanced dressage and less and less on the aids as they become second nature and intuitive. As you do, you'll begin to ride footfalls instead of strides, and your aids will become so subtle they'll be invisible to the onlooker. When this happens, you will quite literally be riding in the moment using the hidden language of dressage.

Section II

Developing the Five

Basics

6 Working With First Tier Basics

*T*he first tier basics are *go, stop, turn in, move out, and soften.* These are "first tier" because every horse has to *go, stop, and turn* to be ridden. A dressage horse also has to *move out and soften.* Another reason I've put these together is that these five basics rely only on each other for training, while everything else in dressage relies on them. Finally, and perhaps most definitively, these are first tier because they — and only they — can be corrected.

Any problems you may be having in training will always be found in one or more of these basics. The measure of your skill in correcting more advanced movements will be in your ability to figure out which first tier basic is the source of the problem and then correct that.

Accepting that everything in dressage comes from these few basics is a radically different way of thinking about dressage. It changes our language and training methods. We no longer think of aids as simply the mechanical application of "hands, seat, and legs." Training becomes a dual process of first getting the horse to understand the concept of each basic and then refining how we ask for it until he "understands" the correct aid combination we use to ask for it.

Aid Combinations

Part of the change to our thinking is acknowledging we always use our aids in combinations of hands, seat, and legs. That we do is patently obvious when you consider that we use our legs to ask the horse to *go*, to halt, and to reinback. Sometimes our legs mean move forward from piaffe to extended trot, other times to go from extended trot to piaffe. We bring our outside leg a little further back to ask for half pass, a canter departure, a flying change, a pirouette, or just to stay on a round circle. This is why the seat and hand are always necessary to give meaning to the legs and why our legs must support hands, and seat. It is only when the three are used in a deliberate, coordinated fashion that a horse can know what we want.

What is not so obvious is that there are very limited aids that can be created by hand, seat, and leg. In fact, when all is sorted out, they can only ask for the five first tier basics. The different movements and figures of dressage are created by sequentially performing the five basics, changing the order and frequency of them as required. For instance, to stay on a round circle the basics might be used in a particular frequency and sequence. To spiral in to a smaller circle, there would be a slight increase in the *turn in* aid relative to the *move out* aid. To spiral back out, there would be less turning in relative to moving out.

Linking aids to the five first tier basics provides a common sense approach for training the horse. For each of the five basics there is an aid and exercises to teach the horse how to react to it. This makes the horse's life much easier — he doesn't have to figure out all of dressage — just the first five basics. He doesn't have to learn different aids to do more advanced exercises later on — he follows the same aids to do more difficult figures and movements as his ability increases.

By linking these few aids to the horse's understanding and response to them, the emphasis is shifted from the rider's application of the aids, to the horse's response. It is no longer a question of the rider using "more inside leg" or "more hand" if things are not going as planned. Rather, it properly becomes a matter of making the horse more sensitive to the rider's aid for the first tier basic at issue. As a result the horse becomes more sensitive to the aids so the rider can use less leg and hand to ride

...the emphasis is shifted from the rider's application of the aids, to the horse's response.

Dual Nature of Training

There is a dual or two part process of training. The first, the cognitive phase, consists of teaching the horse the concept. The second part is teaching him the correct or ideal aids for it. This is, when you think about it, so evident and commonplace it is undeniable. Teaching the horse basic concepts is what makes any reasonably trained horse rideable by any reasonably competent rider. Once a horse understands these basics, which may take some time initially, he can figure out a different rider's aids in minutes if not moments.

The dual nature of training is the reason why I can ride a horse that has been trained by a another person who may be very different from me physically. My aids will never be the same as the horse's regular rider, but they don't need to be. When getting on a horse someone else trained all I have to do is to show him my aid combination or "word" for each of the first tier basics. I don't have to retrain the basics nor do I have to try and match the regular rider's aids with precision.

There are very important ideas to be taken from this.

The first is that it is always more important to use aids in a relaxed way than in a precise way. As long as I'm able to sit in a comfortable, balanced fashion and apply my aids without tension, I can ride any reasonably trained horse reasonably well. If the horse doesn't understand my "aid" for something, I'll use one or more of the exercises I'm about to show you for teaching green horses the five basics. If the horse already understands the underlying concept of the basic, he'll figure out my aid for it very quickly.

...it is always more important to use aids in a relaxed way than in a precise way.

So, if you're ever being told to ride in a way that makes you stiff and tight instead of relaxed and comfortable — you're being told the wrong thing. Your comfort, balance, and relaxation trump any other claim as to what is "correct."

The second idea is that you don't need to use finished aids when teaching the concepts. In fact you don't even want to try to use the "correct" aid at this stage. You're free to move around and make large obvious gestures (big cognitive aids) with your hands, seat, and legs in order to help the horse figure out what it is you're asking for. Later, once the horse understands the concept of the basic, you can refine your aids for it.

For example, when teaching a green horse to turn right, I will open the right rein almost as much as I can while I give and take the rein in a big but not forceful way. To the observer it will look like I'm pointing as if to show the horse where I want him to go and saying, "Hey - come on - let's go over there!" As the horse becomes more familiar with the concept of turning right on request, I gradually make my aids more and more subtle. Eventually, my aid should be so quiet an observer can't see me using it.

The third idea is that I can't tell you with any precision what your aids should be while training the five first tier basics. In coming chapters I will tell you in general terms the aids I use. However, it would be dishonest for me to say this is the way I always do it with every horse or to suggest my example aids are the way you have to do it with your horse.

All experienced trainers will tell you they learn a little from every horse, because each horse is a little different. So, a trainer will always have to modify the aid, the exercise, or both for each horse while teaching each concept. It is only after the horse has the concept that they worry about refining the aid for it.

All of this means the more flexible you are in your approach, the more you observe your horse's responses and adjust technique and methods to suit him, the more you and your horse will learn and the faster you'll make progress. Conversely, the more you stick to the "one true way" the more likely you are to become frustrated and stuck.

The five first tier basics rely on each other for training. You will need *stop* to help teach your horse to *turn in, move out, and soften.* You will find that *turn in* and *move out* help with teaching your horse to *go* correctly. If your horse isn't soft, none of the other basics will be correct, however you can use the other basics to help *soften* your horse. So, play with these and do not become locked into any order. If you're having a problem with one basic, see if you can solve it with another.

The way to train or re-school any of the basics is the Exercise Reward Cycle. We use the Exercise Reward Cycle by first asking correctly with a "cognitive" aid that requests, encourages and allows. Then, if necessary, we correct the horse in a way that may be "mechanical" but must be clear, effective and over with. Finally, we reward immediately and proportionately.

You don't need to use finished aids when teaching the concepts.

As you repeat the Exercise Reward Cycle the horse will begin to understand the cognitive aid. Then he will start to reach out into the hand seeking contact and stretching into his frame as this is the most comfortable way for him to carry a rider. When this happens the aid and the horse will become connected.

Now I'm going to suggest training methods for the five basics and then methods that use the basics to develop movements and figures. These are by no means the only methods and techniques available. I've selected these because they demonstrate an approach to training that is cognitive, bottom up, very gradual, and easy.

The methods in the following chapters are good examples of cognitive, bottom up training that builds on the five basics. These are by no means the only way to train any of these basics, figures, or movements. You are encouraged to experiment with different figures and exercises to accomplish your goals. In fact, the more techniques and exercises you have, the better. As long as you're using cognitive, bottom up methods and progressing in tiny incremental steps, there is a tremendous range of techniques and exercises available to you and your horse.

7 Ground Work

I'M ALWAYS SADDENED when I see a horse and rider locked in an eternal battle of push and pull. The rider who has a top down point of view "knows" the horse should come into a lovely frame and bend evenly through his body as he floats effortlessly across the arena. The rider has been taught it is a matter of finding exactly the right ratio of rein contact, leg strength and "forward" to be able to "push the horse up to bit" as he is "bent around the inside leg." The horse has no idea why humans insist on pulling with their hand and squeezing with their legs, but has been taught, albeit unintentionally, that it's best to ignore this for the hour or so a day he's ridden. They are both the victims of the conventional, top down, mechanical language of dressage.

The two exercises in this chapter are the starting point of cognitive, bottom up training. From this point of view we know that teaching the horse is a matter of getting him to understand one tiny concept after another and then, over time, putting them together. From this point of view it's not a question of using more of an aid, it's always a question of making the horse more responsive to less of an aid.

The two exercises in this chapter are the starting point of cognitive, bottom up training

These exercises are used to help the horse *understand* the first tier basics of *soften* and *move out*. "Flexions" introduces the first tier basic *soften*. It teaches your horse to understand he should accept contact by relaxing the muscles in his jaw, poll, and neck. The second exercise, the "Lateral Engaging Step," introduces the horse to the first tier basic, *move out*. It teaches him how to bend and stretch his body as he moves out. More importantly, it will make him understand that it is easier and more comfortable for him to bend and stretch than to remain stiff.

These exercises are the absolute bare minimum ground work every rider should do with every horse. They are the easiest exercises for both you and your partner, and the most beneficial exercises I know of. I'll show you how to ask your horse to *soften* and *move out* under saddle in those respective chapters later, but for now, here they are from the ground.

Flexions

The first thing your horse needs to know about the bit is that he should "give to it." That's it. Your horse has to understand that he should *soften* in his jaw, poll and neck when you pick up the reins. If he doesn't know this, if he doesn't do this, then he is stiffening when you pick up the reins. If so, you are stuck and will not make progress.

The conventional top down, mechanical approach to making the horse *soften* and reach into the bit correctly is to "send him forward into an accepting hand." It's a nice statement except for the fact that it doesn't often reflect reality.

Horses don't have a top down view. They don't know what is supposed to happen if you do everything just right. They don't think, "Oh, my life will be much easier and more pleasant if I relax and reach out to the bit using all of my muscles correctly." It's way too much to ask them to figure that out in one gulp. It's also way too much to ask of most riders.

The way for most riders to get most horses to understand they should *soften* into the bit is with an exercise called flexions. Flexions are as bottom up and cognitive an exercise as you can get. Flexions meet all the requirements of being a single idea: it is absolutely clear that the horse should *soften*, the single task the horse has to perform is to relax his muscles, and he should do it now.

Flexions also lend themselves wonderfully to use of the Exercise Reward Cycle. The general procedure will be to first ask the horse to *soften* with a correct, or cognitive aid. The cognitive aid is to simply pick up the reins with very little pressure or contact. Then, if you horse doesn't *soften*, you're going to use a correction which may be mechanical, but must be clear, effective, and over with. I'll show you how to put a mechanical pressure in the corner of his mouth in a moment. Finally, when the horse does *soften*, you reward immediately and proportionately.

Flexions also make for a very good example of "immediate and proportional reward." The first time you put a pressure into the corner of the horse's mouth, he's likely to put his head up and just stiffen against your hand for several seconds   perhaps as many as 30 or 40 seconds. Then, if he softens at all, even the tiniest amount, reward immediately by dropping the reins and patting him. As you go on, he'll still take a while to *soften*, but not as long. Still you reward as soon as he gives. Eventually, perhaps several minutes into this, he'll start to give as soon as you pick up the reins. Now you don't reward so soon — instead you will ask him to stay soft for longer and longer.

The reason for the change in tactic is that the horse has changed. A few minutes before, he didn't understand he should *soften* in response to contact. Now, by softening immediately to contact, he is showing he does understand the concept. So, you make a tiny incremental increase in your demand and ask that he stay soft for a little longer.

This goes to the heart of cognitive training. Rather than trying to immediately put the horse into a frame, we slowly teach the horse to simply *soften* to the bit in tiny, incremental steps. In this way he always stays happy and calm, and the result is a horse that knows he'll be happier and more comfortable by simply relaxing into the contact.

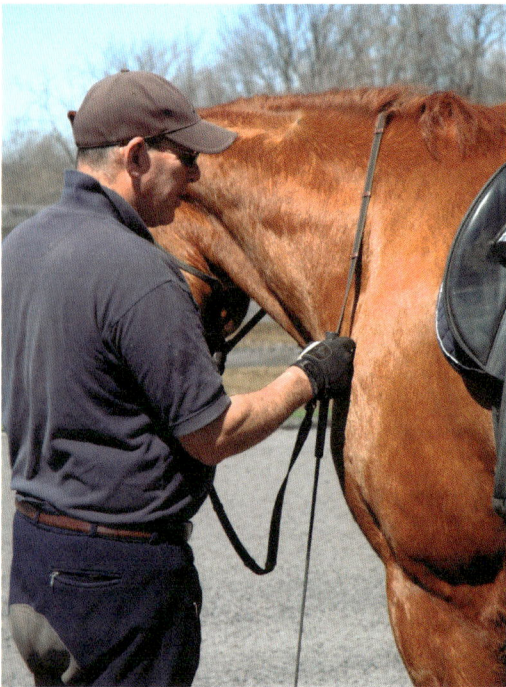

In this series of photos I'm working and bending the horse to the left, so the left side is the inside of the horse, and my left hand is my inside hand. Begin by taking the outside rein in your outside hand, and bring it around so it crosses the neck near the withers. Hold it so your hand is about level with your elbow. Let the weight of your arm create the contact.

Figure 7-1

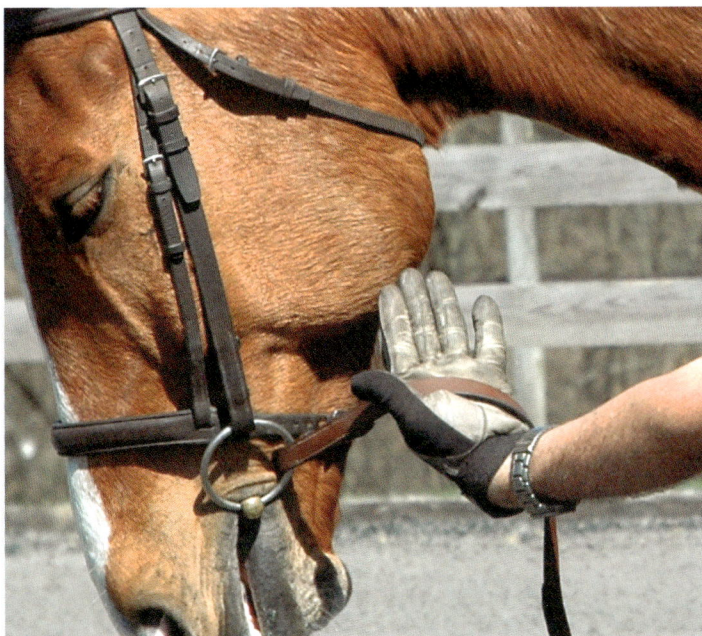

Figure 7-2

Pick up the inside rein as shown, and then rotate your hand so the rein is over the back of your hand and under your thumb. If you begin near the bit and let the rein slide as you bring your hand into position the rein length and contact will be correct when your hand is in position.

Figure 7-3

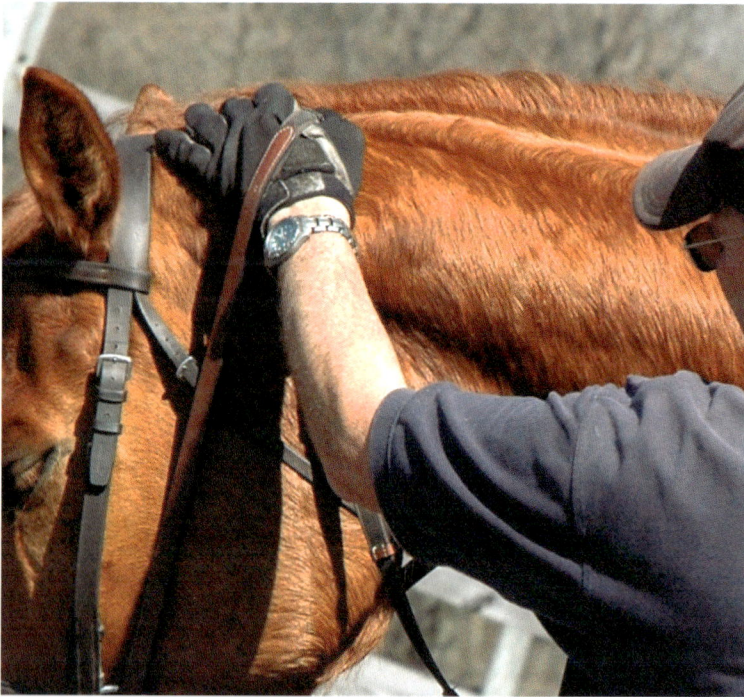

I prefer to put my hand up by the horse's poll as shown in this picture.

Figure 7-4.

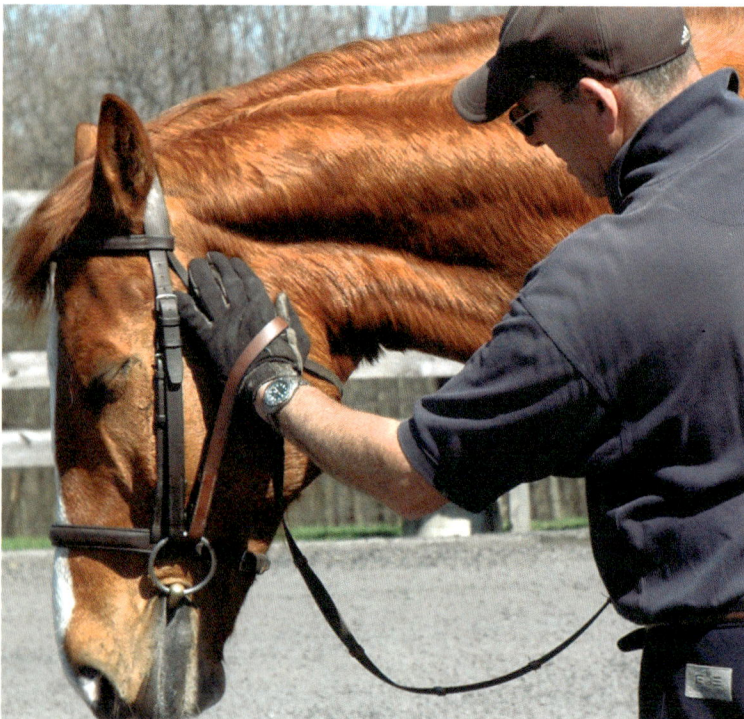

If you find it difficult to reach your horse's poll, bring the rein over the back of your hand and place your fingers on the edge of his cheek bone as shown.

Figure 7-5

Once you have the reins held correctly, pivot your inside hand a little to create a pressure that it is mildly unpleasant for the horse. At first the horse may attempt avoid the contact by bringing his head up, pulling on the reins, twisting his head left or right, and sometimes by backing up. Since you're steadying your hand on his cheek or poll, you'll be able to maintain a steady pressure during all of this. If instead of avoiding the pressure by moving his head, your horse takes a strong hold of the bit and stiffens, vary the contact on the inside rein a little until he begins to relax.

Figure 7-6

Regardless of how the horse reacts at first, eventually he'll relax a little and drop his head. At the very moment he does, even if it's only a tiny barely perceptible amount, release both reins and reward.

In a little time your horse will begin to figure out he should relax and give to the bit rather than stiffen against it. Then he'll begin to relax into the reins as soon as you pick them up. When he does he is beginning to understand and react to the cognitive aid of the very light contact that results from your simply picking up the reins.

Continue to reward as soon as he responds correctly. After a few minutes move on to the next tiny, incremental step in his education. Ask him to stay soft for a moment or two longer before you reward. Do this by keeping the same contact you had on the outside rein, and gently lifting and releasing the inside rein to "play" a little in the corner of his mouth. After you can consistently keep him soft for a few moments, begin to ask for several moments more before you reward.

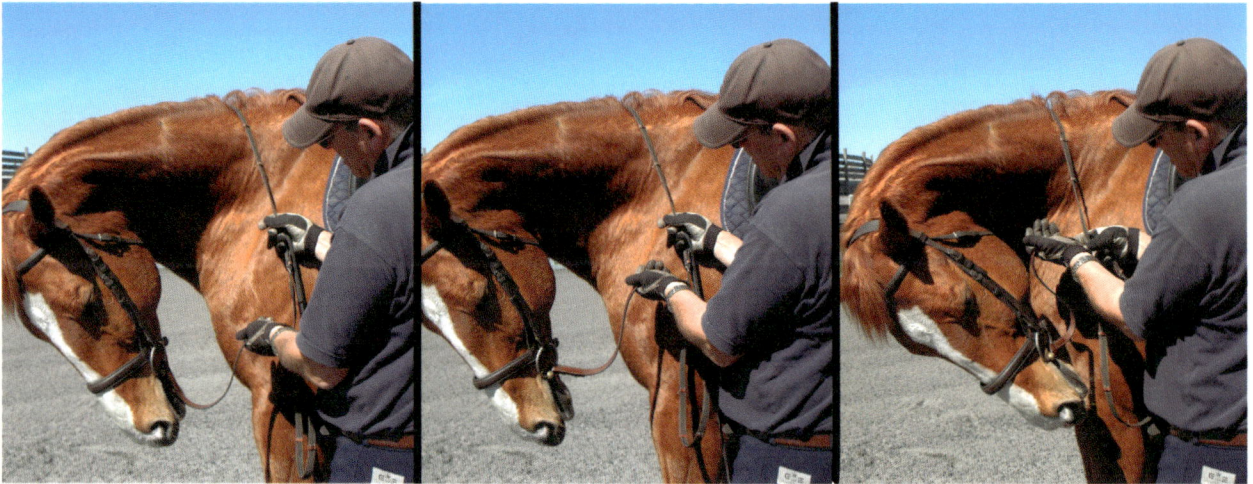

Figure 7-7

Over Bending

When your horse will stay soft easily for several seconds, you can make another tiny, incremental step in his training and ask him to "over bend" his neck. The objective of this exercise is to have the horse release the muscles under his neck near his chest. This is an exercise you would only do very gently, for a few moments at a time, and at the halt.

The proper method is to cognitively teach your horse to increase his bend. Do this by lifting your hand and gently playing with the bit in an upward direction to tease him over. If you do it this way, he will release those muscles just the way he does when he reaches around to scratch himself. The photos above show a horse being gently coaxed around into an over bend that releases his muscles without any backwards pulling or bracing.

If you over bend him mechanically by pulling his head around with the inside rein, he will brace his muscle against the rein — the opposite of what you want.

Releasing Muscle Knots

Most horses, especially those that have been using their muscles incorrectly for years, develop chronic muscle knots in the base of their necks. The shaded area of the drawing shows the where these knots are most commonly found.

If you press your fingers into this area on a horse whose muscles are in knots, it will feel hard, rigid, and bumpy instead of relaxed, soft, and smooth. To release these knots, have him *soften* and bend as just described. Then, while he's still yielding, gently feel along the muscle until you feel a bump. Knead that area as though it were bread dough using your fingers, knuckles, or thumb. Sometimes tapping the muscle with your fingers or hand works well. Each horse is different so experiment until you find what works best with your horse.

At first your horse may be a little sensitive and back away from the pressure you apply, but in just a few minutes he's going to realize that what you're doing feels very good, and start to move into your hand. When this happens let him "tell" you what feels best. If he starts to back away, lighten up, if he moves into you, press back into him until you are both using equal pressure.

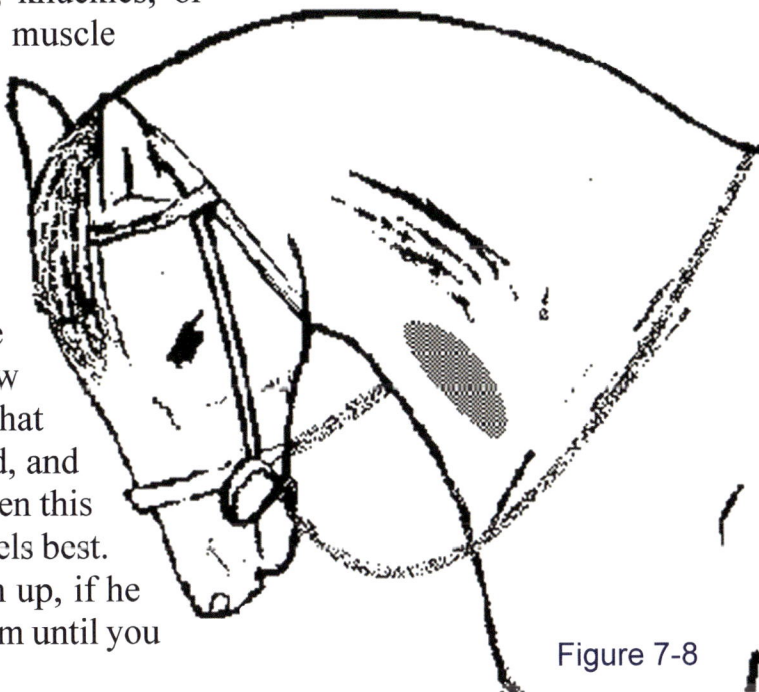

Figure 7-8

Releasing the knots can take anywhere from a few days to a few months. So, until they are released, be sure to massage him daily as you continue with the rest of his training.

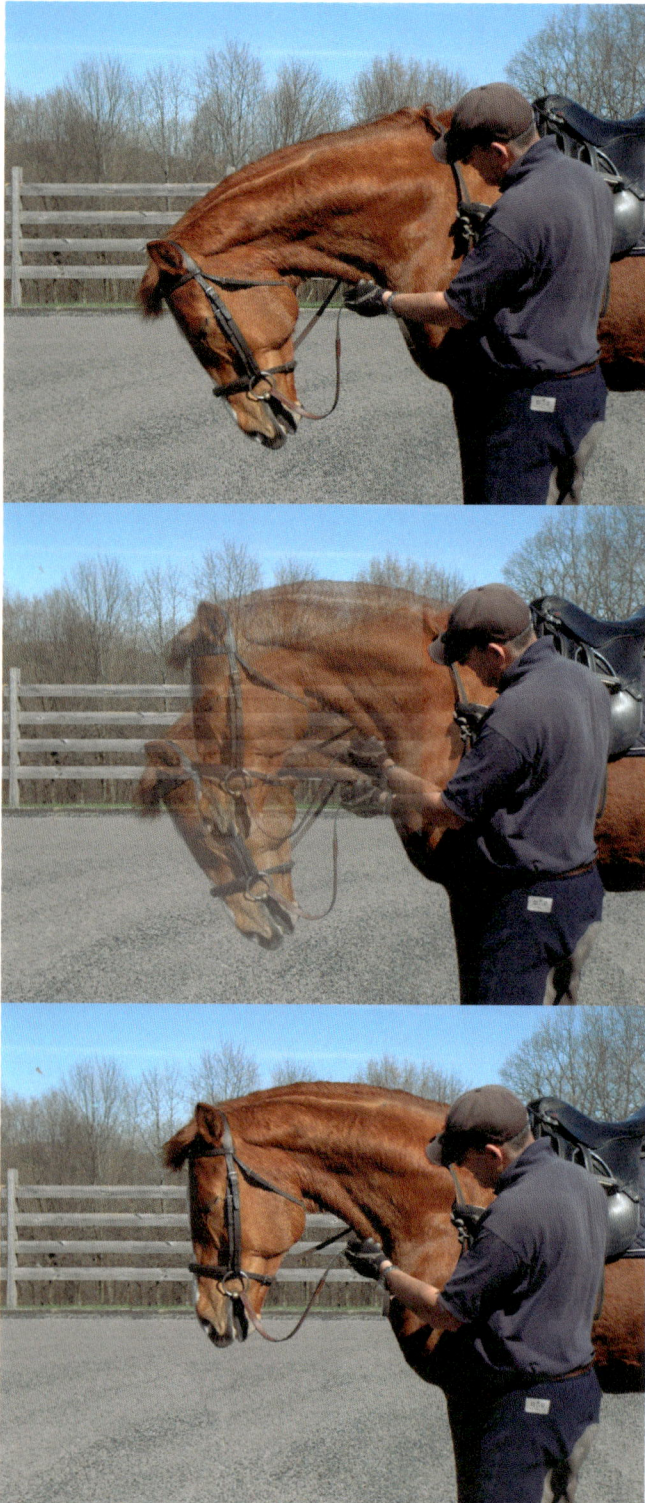

Figure 7-9

Long, Deep and Round

As a result of doing the flexions, bending, and massaging, you should have a soft horse that reaches out to the long and low frame. In that frame the neck should be as long as possible from wither to poll with a nice upward arch in the muscles at the base. The poll should be at or below the level of the withers, loose, relaxed, and at the correct angle.

A poll angle is "correct" when the front of the horse's face will be at or in front of the vertical as the poll elevates to the highest point. In order to "see" the poll at the correct angle when the horse is long and low, you have to imagine it with the neck elevated.

To show you what that would look like, I've digitally removed this horse's head and neck (and my left forearm), rotated it up, and stuck it back on.

The long and low frame provides the best way to physically unlock the horse's back and quarters. Daily work in this frame develops the horse's strength, balance, and agility. Then, as a result of working this way, his poll will elevate — however, that is the last thing I worry about.

The way to properly elevate a horse's poll is to:

Get the horse long and low,

To release and soften the back,

Which allows the horse to engage his quarters,

Which elevates the horse at the wither,

Which in turn causes the horse to raise his head and neck to accommodate the new balance.

Or, you could just pull his head up with your hands, but that's about as effective in getting the horse to engage his quarters as my digital re-balance shown above.

Lateral Engaging Step

The second indispensable ground exercise is the *Lateral Engaging Step*. In this exercise we ask the horse to move laterally with as much bend through his body, stretch over his topline, and crossing of his legs as possible.

As I've already mentioned, we cannot force a horse to bend — not from the ground, and certainly not from the saddle.

Figure 7-10

However, we don't have to force him since we can show him that he will be more comfortable if he relaxes and bends through his body when moving laterally. There is simply no better training method for teaching a horse this fact than this exercise — and there is no other way to get a horse to bend than to teach him this fact.

To prepare for this movement, stand at the horse's shoulder and take up the reins. You can hold one in each hand or both in the inside hand. If you want to hold them both in the inside hand, cross them in your palm as shown in Figure 7-10. Holding the reins this way allows you to feel the horse on each rein and to vary the contact of either.

Begin the exercise by asking the horse to cross just his hind legs as he pivots around you. To do this look towards his quarters as you touch him lightly with the whip either at the hock or just above it.

If your horse's initial response is to kick out at the whip, don't punish him. Ignore it, and keep tapping him with the whip until he either moves away or steps up with the leg being tapped. If your horse just picks his leg up without kicking out, that would be a tiny incremental improvement over kicking out, so reward him for that.

If your horse decides to just walk forward through the reins instead of stepping over or out, you have to *stop* him. If you have both reins in your inside hand and have to *stop* him mechanically, you will probably have to put your outside rein back in your outside hand to do it.

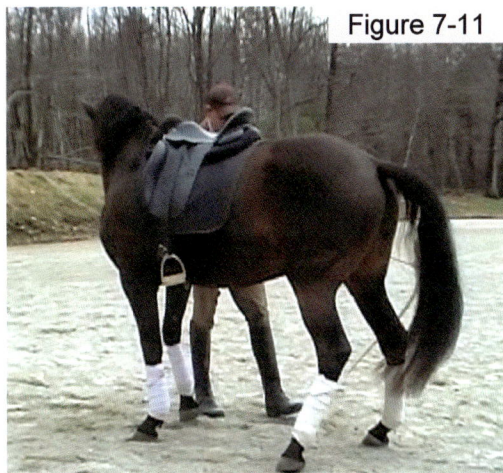

Figure 7-11

When your horse does begin to step away laterally, he will either do it by engaging or by falling out. A horse falls out when he moves laterally by stepping away with the outside hind and then bringing the inside hind over to it Figure 7-11. A horse engages when he bends through his body and crosses his inside hind in front of his outside hind Figure 7-12.

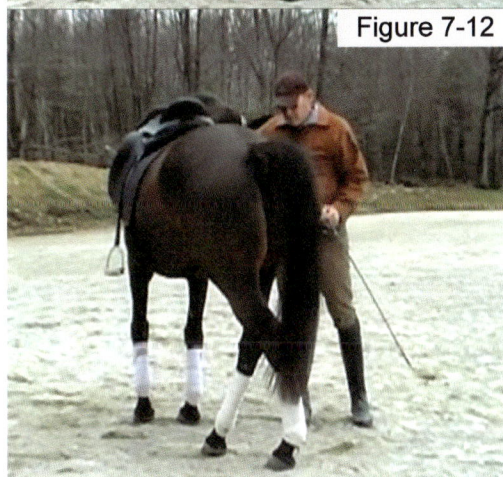

Figure 7-12

It is easier and more comfortable for the horse to move laterally by engaging than by falling out. So, you don't have to try to force the horse to engage. Allow the exercise to teach this to him.

If your horse begins the exercise by falling out, continue it until he takes an engaging step, then reward immediately. The next time I do the exercise he'll probably begin to engage sooner. It won't take him long to figure out what you want and that doing it correctly is easier. When he does, that's just the way he'll do it.

When he consistently crosses in back, the next tiny incremental step in his training is to ask him to move his shoulders away by crossing

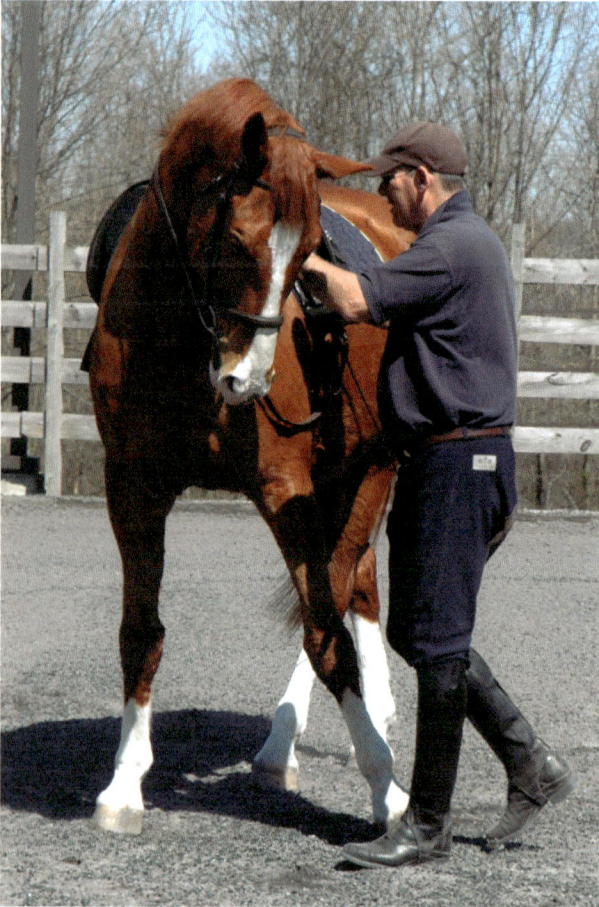

Figure 7-13

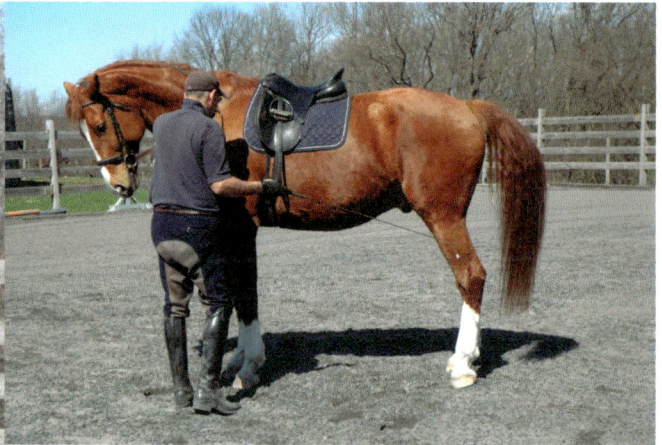

Figure 7-14

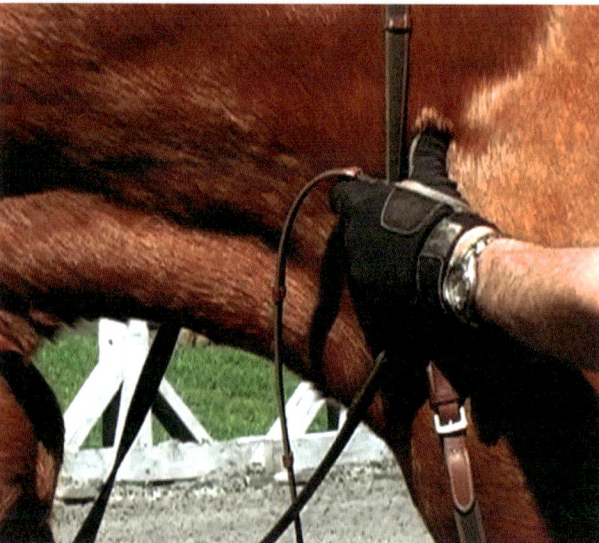

Figure 7-15

his front legs too. There are a couple of little tricks to accomplishing this.

The first is to turn your body so you are perpendicular to him, looking straight across withers (Figure 7-13, 14). If the horse is taller than you, look right at the wither as though you are looking right through it. I am not certain why it is so important to face the wither like this, but it is. Every time I've worked with students having a problem getting the horse to cross his legs in in front and back, I've had them turn to face the wither and the horse begins to cross in front too.

The next detail is to use your thumb or fingers on his neck in the area where you had been massaging his muscle knots (Figure 7-15). This gives him a gentle push or nudge, and reminds him to release his neck which also releases his shoulders.

The third detail is to time your request with the shift in your horse's weight (Figure 7-16).

As your horse is moving his hind legs one after another, his weight will obviously be shifting from inside to outside as he moves. Asking him to move his inside foreleg over while his weight is on it is hopeless and will encourage him to lean on you.

However, if you time your little nudge to when he is shifting his weight away, you'll both find it very easy and natural. This is also an important subtlety for you to develop as a rider — your aids should work with your horse's movement.

Regardless of how advanced a horse is, I start every session with a flexion or two, a quick rub on each side of his neck, and a few lateral engaging steps in each direction. It only takes a few seconds and it sets a good tone for the day's ride.

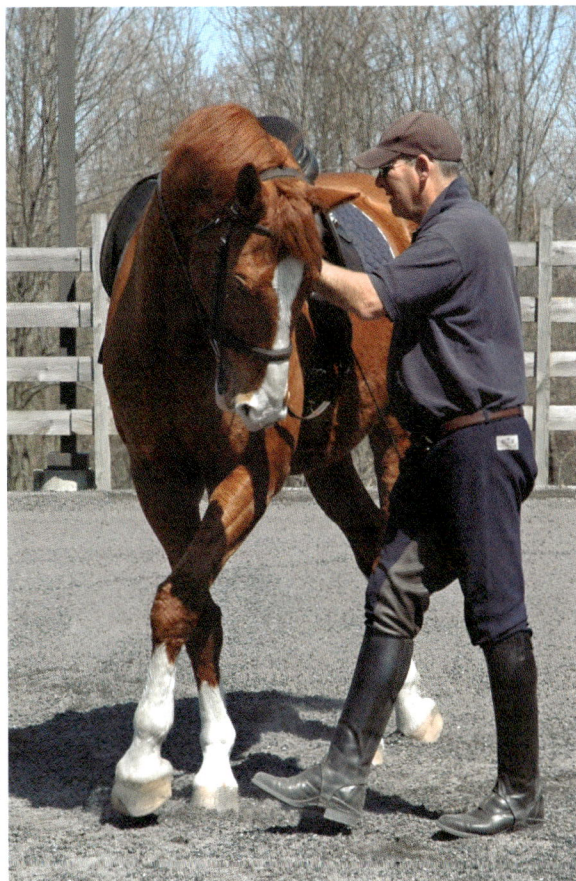

Figure 7-16

8 Go

*A*t first glance, *go* seems easy enough — touch, squeeze, or bump with your legs and your horse begins to move. However, it's not that simple — since *go* is a first tier basic, it must be understood in its cognitive, connected, and mechanical forms.

Cognitive Go

A horse that is doing a cognitive *go* should be on cognitive aids with very little or no contact. The rider should make no attempt to put the horse in a frame or to bend him. The rein contact must be very light and remain essentially the same when the horse begins to move, when he is turning, and when he stops. A horse that is "going" correctly must maintain his tempo without relying on the reins to control his speed.

Connected Go - Moving Forward

A horse that is doing a "connected *go*" is "moving forward." He will maintain an elastic contact, be soft at the poll and have his nose slightly in. His back will be up and flexible. His rear legs will come under his body to lift more than push. *Go* is a first tier basic — "moving forward" results from a combination of first tier basics, training, and conditioning.

Mechanical Go - Riding in a False Frame

When riders try to make their horses do a connected *go* before the horse (or rider) is ready for it, they pull on the reins to hold the horse's nose in, and then use very strong driving "aids" to try and overcome that. There are several flaws with this approach.

The first is that pulling the horse's nose in while asking him to *go* teaches the horse to pull on the reins. Then to turn, stop, or regulate speed you have to pull even harder.

Another issue is that there is no mechanical aid that can force a horse to *go*. Contrary to common belief, there is nothing about squeezing with your legs that makes a horse move. I've demonstrated this hundreds of times by standing in front of a horse while asking the rider to squeeze as hard as he or she can. I've never had to physically *stop* a horse nor have I ever been run over or even knocked out of the way. The explanation for this is simple — the horses understood they shouldn't run me down. So, my mere presence in front of the horse, without any actual physical effort or mechanical force, created a cognitive "don't go" aid that easily overcame the riders strongest efforts to mechanically make the horse move.

It is possible to teach a horse to *go* when you squeeze with your legs, although using a lot of effort has no positive mechanical effect. Worse, squeezing tightens your seat and braces your back which makes it hard for the horse to move his back. This slight mechanical blocking effect is the reason many riders brace to ask horses to halt. So, there is no mechanical *go*, and trying to use one is counter productive.

The Aids

As explained earlier, the precision of the aids is not particularly important. However, it is important that you use your aids in a loose relaxed way. My preference for an ideal *go* aid is to sit up a little, which in and of itself is enough to give a little push with my seat. At the same time I vary the weight of my legs on the sides of the horse.

To vary the weight of my legs, I ride with them hanging from my hips and sinking into the stirrups, as though they were wet towels draped over the horse's back. When I want to vary the weight, I open them just enough that there is less weight from my lower leg pressing in on the horse, but not so much that I take my lower leg off the horse. Then I let the weight of my leg fall back. As you can imagine, this is a very subtle aid! Yet, in comparison to the weight of a fly landing on my horse, which he has no problem noticing, the variation in weight of my leg aid is quite substantial.

Exercises

Note: If your horse is refusing to *go* at all, rearing, bucking, or bolting when you ask him to move off, he is not ready for the work in this book.   I'm assuming your horse will just *go* well enough for you to be safe on him.

Go is a first tier basic, so it relies on the other first tier basics for proper performance. This makes sense when you consider that pulling on the reins to control the horse's speed, to *stop*, and to turn would mean that you would always be pulling on the reins. So, the horse would never have a chance to learn how to *go* on light cognitive contact from light cognitive seat and leg aids.

This seems like another Catch-22 since we're only starting *go* and don't have any other basics yet. You can't teach the horse all five basics first — however, I just said you need all five of the basics to be correct for any of them to be right. The solution to this mystery is not mysterious at all: don't worry about making the basics "correct" early on. Just make each one functional enough to help work on the next.

The way I get the basics functional enough to get started usually begins with me asking him to just start walking — to *go*. With most green or poorly trained horses this means the head will be up, the neck inverted, the back hollow, the stride uneven, and the rhythm and tempo tenuous at best. I don't care. I just need him to move his feet enough that I can give him a quick reward and then ask him to *stop* using the *stop* basic I'll describe in the next chapter.

So, I typically begin by asking him to *go* for a few steps, and then I ask him to *stop*, which you will soon see includes a release and rest for a few moments before I ask him to *go* again. I don't walk for long periods, a few seconds at a time — about long enough to walk a horse-length or two. As I said above, I just need him to move his feet enough that I can ask him to *stop* again.

I say that I "usually begin" with just *go*, because sometimes I have to ask the horse to *turn in* or *move out* for a step or two in order to get him moving at all. Then I can change to a *go* easily enough. In a situation like this, the exercise might look something like the following:

1. I ask the horse to go and get no response.

2. So, I may ask him to turn in or move out since each of these basics has some mechanical elements I can use to get him moving.

3. Once he is moving, I'll try to get him walking straight for a few seconds.

4. After I've let him move long enough that he won't be confused by my asking him to stop, I do ask him to stop. Then, after a short break, I begin again.

Regardless of exactly how I get the horse moving, I'm not trying to fix the walk or the *stop* at this point. I simply want to teach him my cognitive aids for *go* and *stop* so I'll be able to ask for these in a way that doesn't create tension in him or me.

As things progress you and your horse will sort out *go* for trot and canter. I find it's best to begin work in those gaits on your horse's natural circle, which I'll talk about in the chapter on circles.

9 Stop

Stop is a first tier basic, so it must be considered in the cognitive, connected, and mechanical forms. The connected form of *stop* is a halt. I'm not concerned with halt early in training, however, you must have a concept of halt as well as *stop* so you know which you're asking for and why.

In a proper halt the horse maintains his energy as he softens at the poll, brings his back up, and steps under his body with his rear legs. Most horses cannot perform a proper halt early in training because it is a collected exercise that requires preparation and conditioning. Trying to force the horse to halt before he's ready leads to some of the biggest problems in training.

The False, Forced Halt

Trying to force a halt by mechanically holding the horse's nose in while driving the horse's rear legs forward with strong legs is the source of all kinds of problems. It teaches the horse to brace against the hands and fall on his forehand as part of the actual physical process of stopping.

If the contact is released on a horse braced against the hand, he will fall forward and begin moving again. So, in very little time the horse trains the rider to pull on the reins just to keep him stopped. When the rider does want to move, he can't release because the horse's nose will fly up and out. So, he has to be even more aggressive with his legs to get the horse to move at all.

All of this going, stopping, and holding done with strong, restrictive hands and aggressive, tight legs is very harmful. As the horse constantly exercises the wrong muscles in the wrong way, it gets harder for the rider to hold on to him, and harder for the horse just to *go*. As time passes, the rider ends up pushing and pulling more and more for less and less as he and the horse proceed through a downward spiral of ever increasing efforts and rapidly diminishing returns. It's a mess!

You can avoid this mess by teaching your horse to *stop* in response to cognitive aids. This will give him a chance to learn how to step up and re-balance himself without interference. Then the connected *stop*, which is a correct halt, will come easily.

Cognitive Stop

A horse *stops* cognitively when the rider asks him to *stop* and leaves him alone to do it. A correct cognitive aid allows the horse freedom to stretch out into his frame and step up underneath himself as he is stopping. All good riding of every discipline relies on correct, cognitive *stops*.

The method used to teach the horse to *stop* on request is the same method used for all of the first tier basics — the exercise reward cycle. When using the exercise reward cycle you first ask correctly, then, if necessary, make the horse correct, and then reward. The aid used to ask correctly should be a cognitive request that encourages and allows the horse to do what you are asking for. If a correction is necessary, it may be mechanical, but it must be clear, effective, and over with. The reward, as always, should be immediate and proportional.

The correct aid for a cognitive *stop* is to raise your hands a little. Just raising your hands, even a small amount, has enough influence on your seat to create a sufficient seat aid. Do not pull as you bring your hands up. If you had contact before asking for the *stop*, keep the same contact or even *soften* it a bit, as you raise your hands. At this stage don't be concerned with your horse stopping immediately — we're just teaching him the concept of stopping from cognitive aids, so give him some time to figure it out.

As your horse begins to *stop* you must allow him to stretch over his topline and step under with his hind legs. If your horse misinterprets your softening the rein to mean he should keep going, ask again, softening as he begins to *stop* once more. If after two or three repetitions your horse hasn't stopped, you may have to use a correction and just *stop* the horse as if to say — "Hey! When I do this it means you should *stop*!"

As you repeat the *stop* exercise, don't try to fix other things. When you're working on *stop* work on *stop*. Walk forward enough that you're moving and then ask for the *stop* again. If you're going to repeat it, just walk forward a few horse lengths and repeat it. Don't waste time going round and round. The more times you can *stop* in a minute, the fewer minutes it will take for the horse to understand — and he must understand because you need a good cognitive *stop* before you can perfect the other basics and move on.

The following pictures show a horse doing a nice cognitive *stop*.

Figure 9 -1

The horse is just walking along with very little contact.

I ask for "*stop*" with the cognitive aid of just raising my hands a little. Simply raising my hands will, in and of itself, change my seat enough to be effective.

Figure 9 -2

Figure 9 -3.

As the horse *stopped* I dropped my hands to where they were, effectively ending my *stop* aid and letting him step under and adjust his balance to his comfort. If this was a little earlier in his training I would have released the aids even more, probably leaving a loop in the

Corrections — the Mechanical Stop

If your horse does not *stop* in response to your cognitive aids, you'll probably have to use a mechanical correction. This is simply a continuation of the cognitive aid I suggested. Since you have already brought your hands up, bring them up further and sit back more. I also like to push down more in my heel and let my feet move forward. This puts you in a strong secure position and applies strong — but not violent — mechanical force to *stop* the horse.

It is important that if you increase the "aid" into the mechanical correction, you do it slowly enough that the horse has a chance to think about what you're doing and respond. If he does begin to *stop* you must *soften* your aids immediately.

Although it is typical for horses to bring their head up in the early stages of training this, they learn over time to draw the contact out and down as you raise your hands. I explain this more fully in the chapter on "*Soften*."

The following frames show *stop* done with a mechanical correction. This is the same horse as seen above before I taught him to *stop* off my seat.

The horse is walking along on cognitive aids.

Figure 9 - 4

At this point I've asked him to *stop* a few times by lifting my hands while giving and taking the reins. The horse is still not stopping and my hands are already raised to the "cognitive" limit.

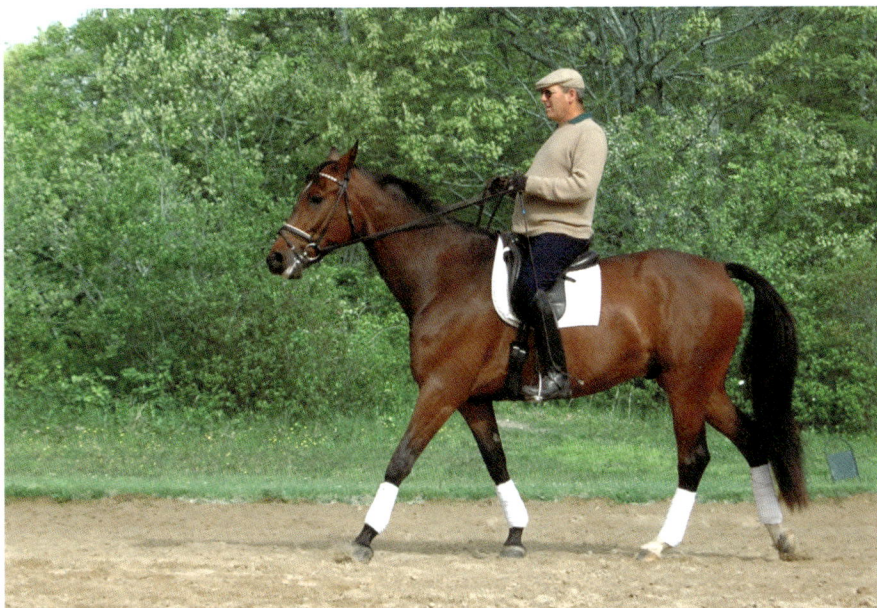

Figure 9 - 5

So, now I'm using a mechanical correction to stop the horse. My "aid" went from cognitive to mechanical when I raised my hands and sat back more. This made it uncomfortable for the horse to keep walking through the bridle. I've put my upper body weight instead of upper arm muscle into the rein by keeping my hands close to my body and my elbows under my shoulders. This way I make the contact heavier without making it rigid.

Figure 9 - 6

Figure 9 - 7

The horse has stopped moving his feet, but still has to readjust his body. So, I let him draw out the contact as he readjusts his frame and weight. I'm passively allowing him to readjust. I'm not assisting or preventing him from shifting his weight. You can see how much he has to shift by comparing the distance between the two lines drawn in this picture and the next.

Figure 9 -8

Fractions of a second later he has adjusted his body forward. The two lines drawn from the back of his foot and point of his rump in this picture are much closer than the same lines in the frame above.

Now the *"stop"* is complete. He has adjusted his weight, relaxed his frame and is just standing there. My mechanical correction of a few moments ago was "clear, effective, and over with". Once the horse learns to do a proper cognitive *stop* he will begin to adjust his weight and frame as he is in the process of stopping. When that happens, his *"stop"* will become a "halt."

Figure 9 -9

Release of the Aids

Regardless of whether your horse stops in response to cognitive aids or if he needed to be corrected, it is important that the rider always "release" the aids after the horse stops and before he is asked to move again.

The release of the aids consists of the rider relaxing or releasing the contact and relaxing his legs so the horse is just standing there, with no physical restriction, waiting for the next instruction.

This has the physical effect of allowing the horse to adjust his balance on his own. It also assures the horse is not being mechanically held in place. In addition, the psychological effect is a very important component of the release. Having the horse stand and wait for his next instruction with no physical restraint is a real exercise in submission. So, whenever schooling any of the five basics, every *stop* should be followed by a release in which the horse stands quietly and waits for the rider to tell him what to do next. This is an extremely important and powerful training tool which only takes a second or so to do but saves years of frustration.

The Halt

As your horse learns to reach out to the contact when stopping, the halt will develop pretty much on its own. If you follow the program outlined here, than one day as you ask your horse to *stop* you'll feel him softening a little in your hand. You'll feel his back come up a little under you. You'll feel the "*stop*" ending with his rear feet stepping up in very distinct foot falls — left! right! When you do, he has just halted rather than stopped.

If you work on the five basics and wait for the halt to start happening on its own, it will — I promise. Then, after you've gotten used to the feeling of a horse stepping up into the halt, you'll find you're able to gently nudge him up to it if necessary. Said in dressage speak, that gentle little nudge is "pushing him up to the bit." Once you've experienced the feeling, you'll realize what a misnomer that phrase is. You haven't pushed at all — merely touched — a gentle nudge that asked, followed by your partner's knowing and willing acquiescence.

10 Move Out

A horse "moves out" when he moves laterally away from the direction in which he is bent — if the horse is bent left he moves to the right. This is similar to the shoulder-in without all of its other qualifications[1]. However, the shoulder-in is only one way for a horse to move out. Moving out is at the heart of almost everything in dressage — this is why the standard description of the aids is, "moving from inside leg to outside hand." We use moving out to teach the horse to bend and then we use moving out to maintain bend in virtually all movements and figures.

Bending through the body while moving out is unique to dressage — no other riding discipline requires it. Yet, it hasn't been defined as a separate, independent entity nor is there a specific exercise to teach this first tier basic. So, I'm coining the term and the exercise "Lateral Engaging Step" to correct that.

---

[1] **Shoulder-in.** This exercise is performed in collected trot. The horse is ridden with a slight but uniform bend around the inside leg of the rider maintaining cadence at a constant angle of approx. 30 degrees. The horse's inside foreleg passes and crosses in front of the outside foreleg; the inside hind leg steps forward under the horse's body weight following the same track of the outside foreleg, with the lowering of the inside hip. The horse is bent away from the direction in which it is moving. (USEF DR 111-3 f.)

The Lateral Engaging Step Under Saddle

The lateral engaging step is a first tier training exercise in which the horse is asked to move laterally with as much bend, stretch and crossing as possible. The goal of the exercise is to teach the horse that it is easier for him to move laterally by bending and stretching into the reins. When it can be done easily and effortlessly in both directions, the horse is "laterally supple". For any horse to be "on the aids" he must be proficient at this exercise.

Traditionally, the basic skill of moving from the inside leg to outside aids is taught as part of more advanced exercises. For instance, the shoulder-in requires this, but it also requires a degree of collection, impulsion, constant tempo, rhythm, steady contact, and an even bend from poll to dock. Certainly we want to end up with all of these qualities, and it is possible to get them all at once with highly skilled hands. But shoulder-in is a more difficult and demanding way for a horse and rider to learn them. So I use the Lateral Engaging Step because it's easiest way to teach horse (and rider) some of the most important skills and feelings there are in dressage.

It is possible to teach the horse this exercise from the saddle, however, it's best to first do it from the ground as described in the chapter "Ground Work."

The Lateral Engaging Step provides an exercise that can be done in isolation. There is no need for impulsion, tempo or rhythm. There is no particular place (dressage ring letter) to do it. This is a slow easy exercise that gives you the chance to feel your horse shifting his weight, moving and bending under you. As he gets better at it and enters the connected stage you'll have the opportunity to feel the correct, soft contact of a horse reaching into your hands. Its form follows its function which is to show the horse the easiest way to do the exercise is to bend and move away from the rider's inside leg into his outside hand. By practicing it this way, you are soon able to incorporate it into every figure and exercise.

The Aids

The ideal aids for the Lateral Engaging Step are inside leg touching lightly at the girth asking the horse to move into a receiving outside rein. The rider's belly button and nose should be pointed along the outside of the horse's neck.

The rider's inside hand brings the rein forward and up in the direction of the horse's inside ear. When first teaching the exercise the movement of the hand may be a quite dramatic big cognitive aid. Later, as the horse begins to understand what is required the rein aid should be barely perceptible.

The outside hand provides a contact for the horse to move into by drawing straight back as a direct rein. The outside leg is back slightly and passive. If the horse begins to run through the outside aids, simply stop the horse after each step. Soon he will understand he should go to, but not through the outside aids.

Mechanical phase

In the mechanical phase, begin by asking the horse with light cognitive aids to move over. Most horses will make the mistake of just going forward instead of moving over. When he does, stop the horse, then release the aids, wait a moment and begin again. Most horses will try moving over instead of forward after a few tries.

If he doesn't get the idea or move at all after a few attempts, you can make him correct by just mechanically pulling him over a step or two. Do this by lifting the insider rein higher with more force, and drawing back more strongly with the outside rein. You can also tap him with the whip on the inside. After a few cycles using this method he should definitely get the idea. However, if he doesn't you will have to get off and school him from the ground as shown in the "Ground Work" chapter.

Cognitive

When the horse begins to move away from your light cognitive aids, no attempt is made to bend the horse or to put him "on the bit". If he brings his head up, you should, as always, bring your hands up so they are not lower than the horse's mouth, but that's all you should do with them. Follow his head up so your hands remain level with his mouth, but make no attempt to make the horse bend and soften. You must allow the horse to figure out from doing the exercise that his life is easier when he bends and softens.

When first doing the exercise, reward as soon as he steps over instead of forward. After a while, when you're confident he knows to move over instead of going forward, you can ask for more strides. Soon you'll find that he begins to soften as he moves over and you should immediately reward that when he does. With careful repetition you'll notice that he begins to soften and bend sooner and sooner and more and more each time you do the exercise.

Connected

Soon, he'll begin to bend and soften as you ask for the movement to begin. You now have effectively taught your horse to bend away from your inside leg. Note that you had to go through the training process to teach him to bend away from your leg — there is no mechanical force of your leg that can make him do that.

The following series of pictures show a typical run through the Lateral Engaging Step. I had already asked this horse to move away from one leg and than the other dozens of times, and he hadn't yet shown much interest in softening as he did it. However, the camera captured the moment when he discovered how much easier his life is when he bends and softens in the exercise.

This series shows how progress can be measured in moments (as opposed to days, weeks, months or years) when you slow down, relax, and allow your horse to learn how to do what you want instead of trying to make him do what you want. Although this series caught a good moment for this horse it is definitely not a unique moment in terms of training horses this way. These epiphanies are common place when training with these methods.

Figure 10-1

Typically, a horse will make the mistake of just going forward or backing up when you ask him to move over. If he does, just stop him, release the aids, wait a moment, and then ask again.

Figure 10-2

After a while he will begin to get the idea that he should move over and away from the leg instead of just running forward. In this picture I've just touched him lightly with my right leg. He has responded by trying to step over with his right hind (the leg wrap is tinted blue in this series of pictures for clarity). This is a fairly standard early attempt in that his head is up, his back is hollow and stiff. As a result the movement is rigid and there is very little crossing.

If this was one of the first times he had moved away instead of trying to run through, I would have rewarded him for just this step, stiff as it is, and then begun again.

Figure 10-3

Within the same stride he has begun to drop his head slightly but remains stiff and rigid as he tries to step over with his front leg. The result is this pitiful little step in which he is barely able to get his right foot in front of his left.

Still, it is clear by the loose rein that he understands he should move over and not run through my hand. This lets me give him all the freedom he needs to figure out the easiest way to move over.

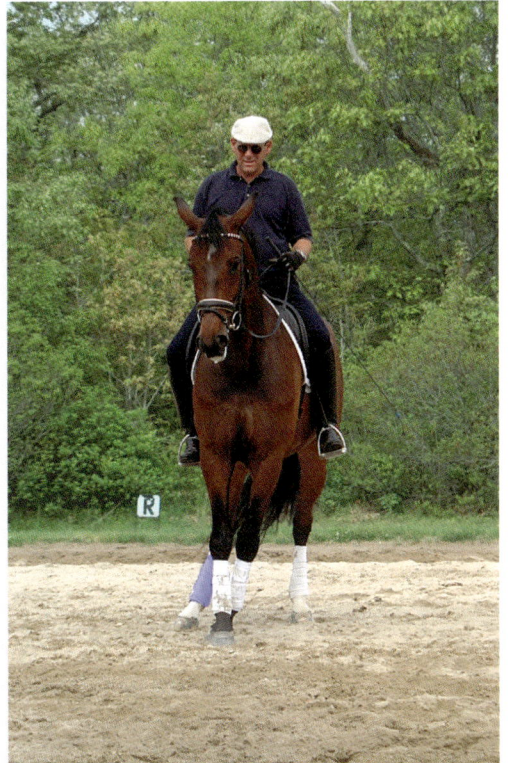

Figure 10-4

In the very next stride, he is starting to bend through his body. As a result the movement is becoming easier for him and he is able to cross his right hind more than in the previous stride.

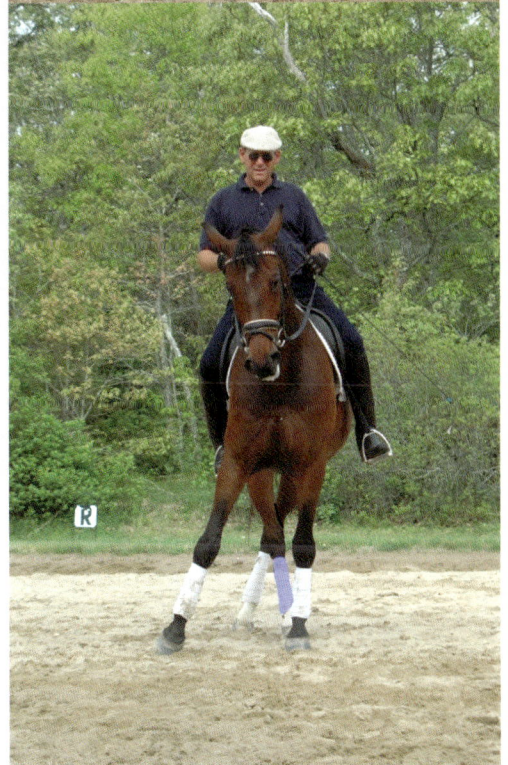

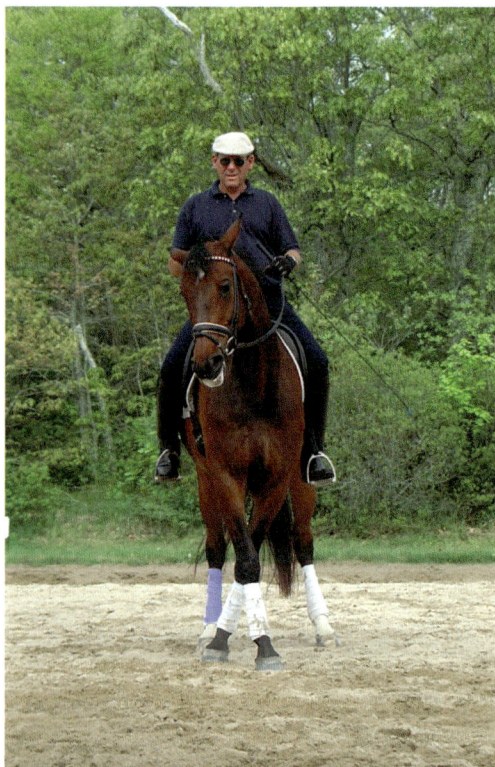

Figure 10-5

Now, because he is not as rigid and stiff as he was in the last stride he is able to bring his right front much further over. This improvement is the result of him bending a small amount but he still hasn't begun to stretch.

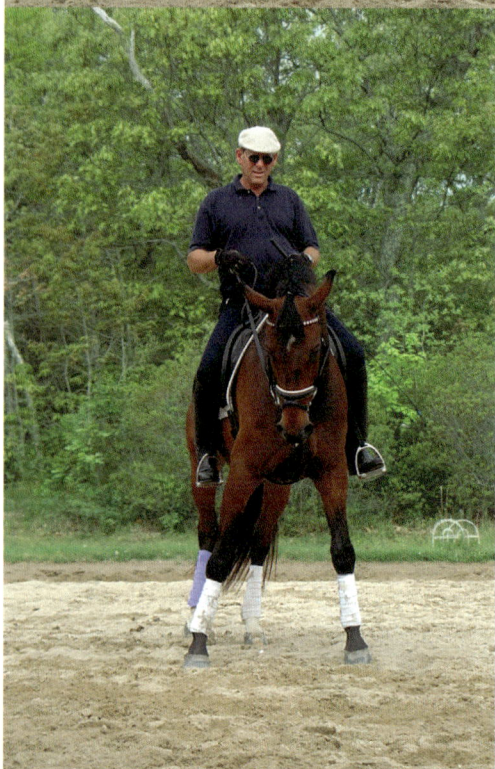

Figure 10-6

Less than second later he has decided to try stretching out to my hand. Look how much lower his head is now!

Figure 10-7

Here he continues to make the transition from the cognitive stage to the connected. He is reaching into both hands making his neck as long as possible from wither to poll. His poll is clearly lower than I want to end with, but riding him out and round like this is the perfect antidote for the stiff, hollow backed horse I had just three strides ago.

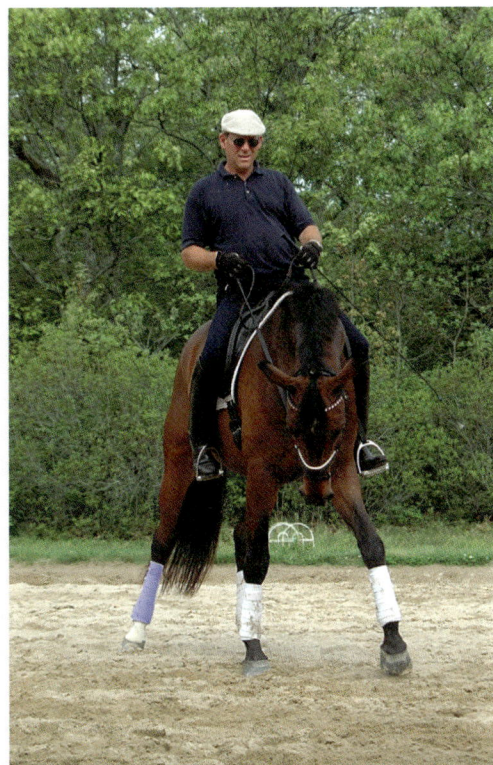

Figure 10-8

And finally, as he steps over with his right hind, he bends throughout his body as he stretches over his top line to my hands. His body has gone from rigid, stiff, and awkward to loose, supple and elegant. His stride has gone from choppy and pathetic to long and fluid.

Now that I have started these qualities of looseness, calmness, and confidence I want to be sure to never, ever lose them again. There is nothing more important and any time he begins to lose these qualities I will return to simple easy exercises like this to get them back before worrying about anything else.

Figure 10-9

There is still another significant improvement to be achieved from this exercise. Up to now the horse has been softening and bending as a result of doing the exercise. The next goal is to have him soften, bend and stretch into hand in anticipation of the exercise. These pictures show precisely this.

Here I've finished moving the horse away from my right leg. I'm getting ready to start moving him from my left leg

Figure 10-10

As I gently touch him with my left leg he begins to straighten and then bend and shift his weight to his new outside in anticipation of moving in the new direction.

Figure 10-11

In this picture he has shifted his weight to his right side and changed his bend from right to left. Note that his feet have not moved at all in these pictures.

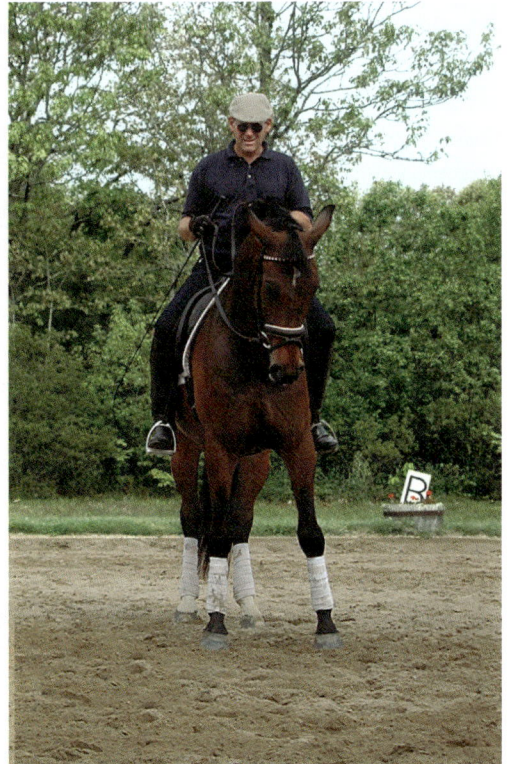

Figure 10-12

In this moment the horse has an even bend from poll to dock and has shifted his weight to his right legs. This has freed his left foreleg which is just beginning to come off the ground.

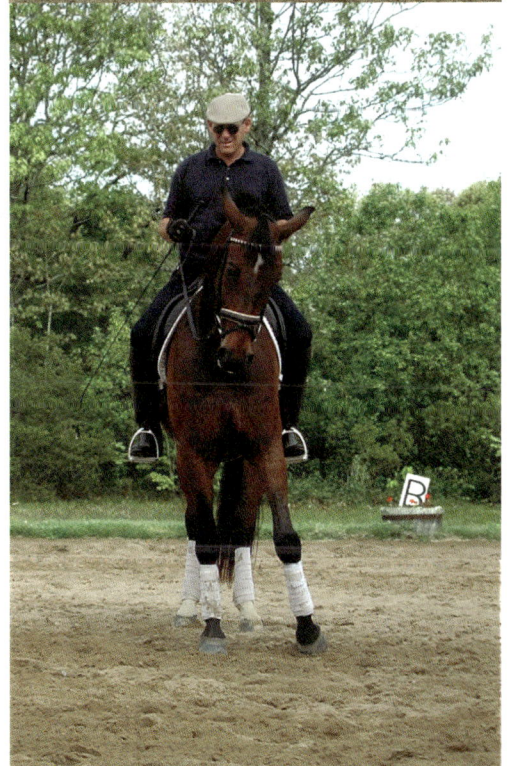

So, having done the Lateral Engaging Step exercises for several dozens of times over two days, the horse will "bend away from my leg." Note this is a learned response. There is no mechanical way to bend a horse — he either knows he should and does in response to your request, or he won't. Trying to accomplish this result mechanically by using "more leg" only makes both horse and rider "more stiff". Without teaching your horse to respond to your leg this way, he'll never be on the aids and you will not ever be able to do dressage.

11

Turn in

*T*he term *"turn in"* as I use it refers to changing a horse's direction by bringing his shoulders, and to a lesser extent his quarters, into the direction of his bend. Teaching the horse the first tier basic *turn in* also teaches him to let his shoulders and quarters be contained or controlled by the outside rein and the rider's outside leg.

I call the exercise used to train the first tier basic *turn in* a "schooling turn." The form of the schooling turn falls somewhere between a large turn on the haunches, and a small haunches-in on the circle. Although previously unnamed, this type of exercise in its many variations is commonly used. The formal dressage movement that comes closest to the schooling turn is the turn on the haunches. However, the turn on the haunches comes with a variety of other qualifications[1]. So, trying to use it to teach the first tier basic brings us back to the pervasive Catch-22 — in order to use the exercise to put your horse on the aids, your horse must be on the aids. This is why the schooling turn is used initially while training the horse to

---

[1] DR112 - 9. The Turn on the Haunches. This movement is a schooling exercise which can be executed from a halt or walk and is preparatory for the pirouette which is executed out of a collected gait. The horse's forehand moves in even, quiet and regular steps around the horse's inner hind leg while maintaining the rhythm of the walk. In the half turn on the haunches the horse is not required to step with its inside hind leg in the same spot each time it leaves the ground but may move slightly forward. Backing or loss of rhythm are considered a serious fault. This movement may be executed through 90 degrees, 180 degrees, or 360 degrees.

turn in. As he makes progress, you can proceed to the turn on the haunches and other more advanced lateral movements.

The Aids

Begin by bringing your inside hand forward and upward towards the horse's inside ear, to flex the horse to the inside. If you've done the flexions exercise from the "Ground Work" chapter your horse should be familiar with this. How much you flex the horse and how forward and up you bring your hand depends completely on how much flexion the horse you are riding needs. Early in training you may have to flex him a lot by bringing your hand very noticeably up and forward. As your horse improves, the aid and flexion should be barely perceptible.

Turn your upper body a very slight amount — so slight that you do not twist in the saddle, but merely re-direct your upper body. This will change your weight but not your position. As this part of the aid has no mechanical effect, the amount you twist or turn your upper body does not vary depending on how well the horse is going.

Bring your outside leg back and tap lightly. This has no mechanical effect regardless of how hard you squeeze or kick so you might as well teach your horse to respond to a light touch. Draw your outside hand straight back — do not bring it over the withers and mechanically pull him in the direction you want. Remember to release and reward as soon as the horse does a step or two.

The ideal aid to ask a trained horse to *turn in* is essentially the same as we use to turn ourselves while walking — we simply turn our belly button to where we want to go. This is how little effort it should take to correctly ask a horse to *turn in*. Just turn yourself a slight amount — so slight that you do not twist in the saddle, but merely re-direct your upper body. This will change your weight but not your position in the saddle.

If you keep your outside hand in front of your belly button, this is, or should be, enough of an outside rein aid. The inside rein can be opened slightly by rolling your hand to bring your thumb out. Your outside leg should be used gently as a signal to him, but remember that it has no mechanical effect and using a lot of effort doesn't help.

Development

I am always using what I learned in the last attempt to make this one a little less terrible.

I like to work these early exercises on a roughly shaped square. I walk up to any place, *stop*, release the aids, and then ask the horse to *turn in* for a step or two. At first I don't expect very much at all. Usually the horse will try to walk straight through, do a turn on the middle, or sometimes even back up a few steps. I don't care. As long as I end up with him turning in a step or two, I'm satisfied. Then, no matter how bad it was, I'll walk up a few feet to my next corner. Once there I'll *stop*, release, begin again. Using the square this way, each corner becomes a single repetition of the Exercise Reward Cycle.

Yes, I do end up with some very funny looking squares initially. That's fine — I'm only trying to give my horse the idea of what's expected. Things will be refined as we go on. Since I'm working on a square, I'm under no pressure to make the horse do the exercise with precision. I'll be in another corner of my small square in a few seconds and I get to try again then. Yes, my ultimate goal is to someday, in the far-off future, do the *turn in* so well that I'll get a good mark for canter pirouettes. However, right now, in this moment, my only goal is to do the *turn in* a little less terribly than I did a few moments before.

This is the essence of cognitive training — I'm not trying to make the horse do a good *turn in* now. I am trying to help the horse understand what I want so that later he'll do the exercise very well in response to light, non-restrictive aids. As with all cognitive training, when I ask the horse to *stop* I always release the aids and have him stand for a few moments waiting for my next instruction.

A typical session to introduce a horse to this exercise might go something like this. I walk up to the first corner of my square, *stop*, and release the aids. Then after a moment I ask the horse to *turn in* a step or two. It is not uncommon for the horse to walk straight ahead instead of turning in. So, I *stop* him, wait a moment, and then ask again. This time instead of bringing his shoulders in the horse may throw his quarters out. That's fine, as long as I'm pointing roughly towards the next corner of my square I've done the exercise. So I have him walk a few strides to the next corner, *stop*, release, and begin again.

Keeping in mind that in the last corner he threw his quarters out instead of bringing his shoulders in, I'll adjust my aids to help make it clearer for him. I might move my outside leg back a little further, or keep him straighter in his body. It's reasonable to try counter bending him a little to see if that helps. He and I will muddle our way through this corner, hopefully, but not necessarily, being a little less terrible than we were in the last corner. At the next corner I'll make any adjustments I think necessary and try again. Working in this casual way, I'm not trying to fix what has already happened and I'm not trying to force him to do it right. I'm always using what I learned in the last attempt to make this just a tiny bit better.

Once horses start to figure out the exercise, it is common for them to rush through the movement. In this situation I'll *stop* the horse after each step, release the aids, and then take another step. So, I could end up stopping and releasing my horse 3 or 4 times to make one 90 degree turn, but that's fine as long as he learns to turn easily without rushing or leaning on the reins.

While I just gave a few examples of corrections, it is typical to have to figure out different solutions for each horse. It's also normal to try things that don't work or are not helpful. Not a problem — learn what you can from it and go on to the next corner. The only thing that is certain is that if you keep getting a little bit better, pretty soon you'll be pretty good.

Figure 11-1 shows the *turn in* exercise on done on a square. It also shows a progression from the first few attempts of the *turn in* exercise to a finished form that would be typical of a horse ready for walk and canter pirouettes.

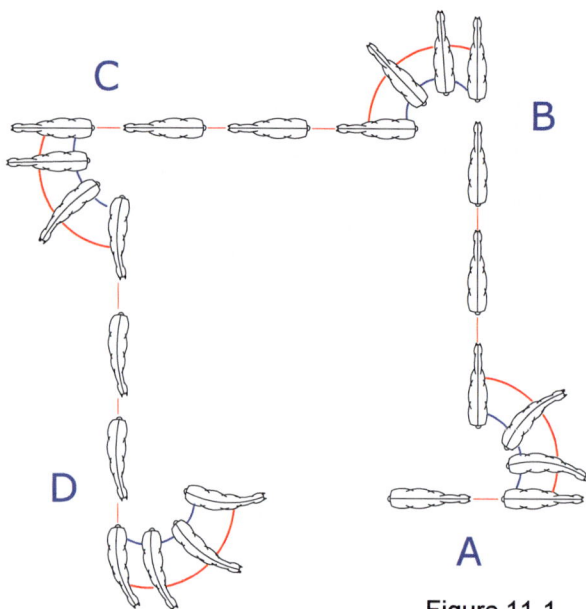

In this diagram you see the horse in four stages of learning to *turn in*. The first corner -A- shows how a horse brand new to the exercise may perform it by counter bending. -B- shows a horse that is "getting the idea" — he doesn't need to be counter bent, but he isn't bending into the exercise yet either. -C- shows a horse just learning to bend as he does the exercise and -D- shows how a fairly advanced horse ready to school actual pirouettes would do the exercise. Although I've shown the progression in just one square, in practice it would take many dozens or even hundreds of repetitions of the exercise to get to this advanced stage.

Figure 11-1

There is nothing mandatory about training the *turn in* on a square — I've just found it a convenient shape to teach both horse and rider. I like that it gives me many opportunities to have the horse do the exercise, and then, after walking straight ahead a few steps, to repeat it. I usually keep the square roughly parallel to sides of ring and far enough from the walls that there is room for the exercise.

When your horse begins to anticipate the *stop* at each corner, you don't have to fully *stop* anymore. Simply approach the next corner and "almost *stop*". If your horse *softens* as he prepares to *stop*, you may proceed to *turn in* as though he had *stopped*. This is a significant improvement because he has performed a rudimentary half-halt.

Once *turning in* most horses will figure out the easiest most comfortable way to do the exercise is by bending into the turn, stretching over the topline into the outside rein. Of course, not all horses figure this out as quickly as others. An option to use with them is to do a full circle, or more at each corner until the horse begins to *soften* into the exercise. In this variation, allow him to *stop* or walk off as a reward as soon as he begins to *soften* and stretch.

Here are some pictures of a horse doing a pretty good *turn in*.

In this photo I've just begun to ask the horse to *turn in* from the track.

Figure 11-3

In this moment you can see the horse is still stepping well up as he brings his shoulder in from the track.

This frame provides a very good angle to see my aids. My inside hand is slightly open and leading — but not pulling — the horse to the inside. My outside hand is directly in front of my upper body which is pointed over the horse's inside shoulder towards his inside ear.

Figure 11-4

Figure 11-5

In this moment you can see the horse remaining soft and reaching as he allows the outside rein to guide his shoulders in and over.

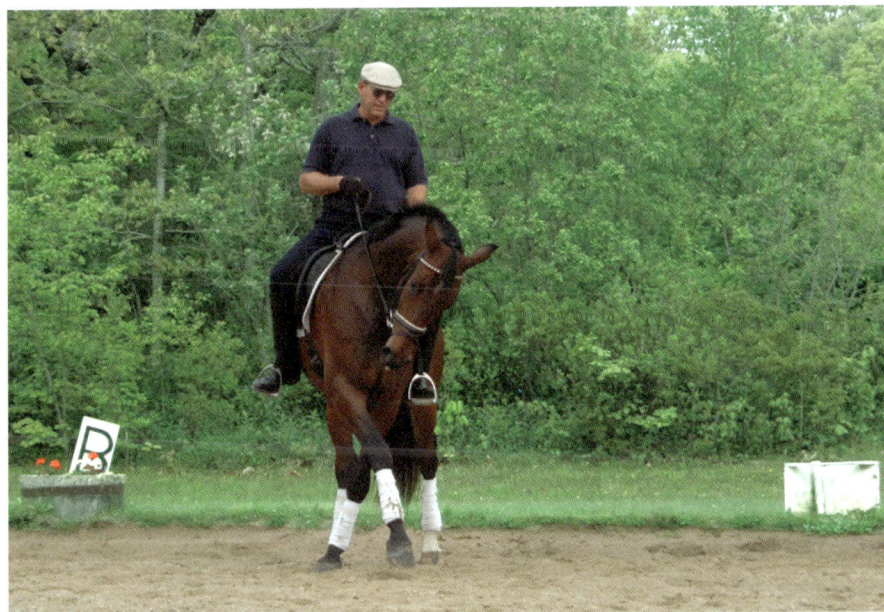

12 Soften

A soft horse is physically supple, elastic and free of tension in his body. A soft horse is free of mental tension as he accepts the rider's leadership and performs with willing compliance. A soft horse moves with relaxed muscles, lengthens his frame by stretching over his top line, and bends to one side by stretching the other. If you release the inside rein of a soft horse, he will maintain his bend, frame and tempo.

The opposite of a soft horse is one that is stiff, bracing or pulling. A stiff horse has unnecessary tension in his body which makes it hard for him to move. A rider can mechanically hold a stiff horse in a frame and bend his neck by pulling on the reins. However if the rider releases the inside rein the horse will lose his bend and frame.

Making dressage horses soft in a way that stretches is not new. What I'm simply calling *soften* would, in dressage speak, involve long discussions of "suppleness," "elasticity," "forward," and "engagement." I have just put them into a single word.

Contact

Having all these qualities linked works very well with the idea that the contact is correct when the horse reaches more into it. A horse is reaching into the contact when the muscles under his neck remain relaxed as his neck gets slightly longer over the top all the while maintaining a loose, relaxed poll. He then moves comfortably into bit and the contact is correct. There is no stiffness or rigidity anyplace. Rather it feels a little like a rubber band, mid range between no tension whatsoever or pulled so tight there is no more stretch.

On a trained horse, obtaining correct contact should be no more difficult than gently taking the slack out of the reins. As the horse feels the initial light touch of the bit he will respond by reaching into it as I've just described. It is this simple.

However, with a green or poorly trained horse, it will usually require considerable training to teach him to respond this way. I say "usually", because very skilled riders can, and often do, jump on a horse and "send it forward" as they cognitively teach the horse to *soften*, and then begin to have it connect, bend, reach, engage in what appears to be a single process that only takes a few minutes. Unfortunately, when most of us mere mortals attempt this we end up teaching the horse to stiffen and pull on our hands. So, most of the time, most riders will have to go through a training process to teach the horse to *soften* as he stretches.

Developing Softness

The process of teaching the horse to *soften* and stretch into the bit begins with his initial response to bit. This response can be stated as a single idea in just 3 words, "Give to it."

That's it. The single idea for the first tier basic of *soften* is "give to my hand." More precisely the first tier basic of *soften* consists of the horse yielding to any pressure put on the bit by relaxing their jaw, poll, and the base of their neck. The absolute best bottom up, cognitive approach to teaching this is with the flexions exercise I discussed in the chapter on Ground Work.

The best way to teach a horse to *soften* and stretch through his body is with Flexions and the Lateral Engaging Step which I have already shown in the chapters on ground work and "moving out." You should do those exercises from the ground before you ask your horse to *soften* under saddle!

Soften Under saddle

Before asking your horse to *soften* under saddle it's absolutely necessary to have him doing very nice"*go*", "*stop*", and "turn-in" in response to cognitive aids. If your horse is not stopping and turning to feather light seat and rein aids then you are stopping and turning him by pulling on him — the antithesis of softening.

When you insist the horse goes precisely where you tell him to on light aids, there is no incentive for him to pull. If you ride on non-restrictive aids, and immediately *stop* him every time he veers off the path you have selected (or when you feel him stiffen on the rein), he will soon realize the futility of trying to pull through. By simply deciding you are going to use aids you're comfortable with and the horse is going to listen to them or be corrected every time he doesn't, you will make a light horse that will be easy to teach to *soften*.

The opposite of stopping and correcting your horse when he tries to run through your aids is to keep him going and using more hand or more leg to keep him on track. By allowing your horse to continue when he pulls on you, you're teaching him to pull on you. You're also teaching him to remain stiff and against you. Obviously, you can never make him soft if you're teaching him to be stiff.

The following series of pictures shows a mounted softening exercise. It is essentially the ground exercise "flexions" done under saddle. These pictures were taken at 1/3 of a second intervals so you can see this should be a dynamic exercise in which the horse softens almost immediately, not a tug of war in which the horse continues to brace.

At the moment shown in Figure 12-1 the horse is bracing against the rein instead of softening to it. So, I brought my hands up and apart to put a gentle pressure into the corners of his mouth. Because I had already done flexions from the ground with him, he knew he could relieve the pressure by relaxing and putting his head down.

Figure 12-1

I responded to his raised head with a cognitive rein that followed his head up but does not mechanically restrain him from reaching forward into the contact.

Figure 12-2

1/3 of a second later he is already beginning to *soften* and reach down into the bit instead of pulling further back and away from it.

Figure 12-3

At 2/3'rds of a second you can see the horse continues to reach down and I follow him with the same contact I started with..

Figure 12-4

A full second later the horse's frame is good but he's a little stiff at the very base of his neck. So, I raised my hands just a bit to increase the pressure and encourage him to release that last little bit....

Figure 12 -5

As I continue to work with this horse I will want him to continue to *soften* as he reaches further out and down.

Figure 12-6

Which he did so I released the reins and rewarded him.

Figure 12-7

Eventually he should be so willing to softly draw out the contact that I can either *go* along with him taking a nice reaching contact like he is in this picture....

Figure 12 - 8

or I can have him lengthen his neck and stretch down as he is here, a few seconds after the above picture was taken.

Figure 12 -9

Kathy Von Ertfelda shows her fully trained horse Talento reaching softly out and down to the bit in their daily warm-up.

Figure 12-10

A few minutes later she shows a passage that is as soft, relaxed, and expressive as you will ever see. Collection this elevated and easy is only possible on a horse that is absolutely free of tension in his body and mind.

Section III

Working With the Basics

13 Developing the Circle

*I*N THIS CHAPTER you'll see how the five basics are used to develop a circle, and how to correct the most common problems riders have on circles. In addition, I will introduce a concept I call the "Natural Circle" and you'll learn how to use these cognitive exercises to create true connection.

The first exercise used to develop a circle is a figure I call the "turning square." In this exercise the horse is asked to do the *turn in* exercise, walk a few steps, and then repeat the *turn in* exercise. The horses in corners A & B of this figure represent that.

In a slightly more advanced version of the exercise, the horse is asked to *turn in* and then *move out* a few steps along the side of the square and then to *turn in* again.

The horses in C & D of this diagram show what that looks like.

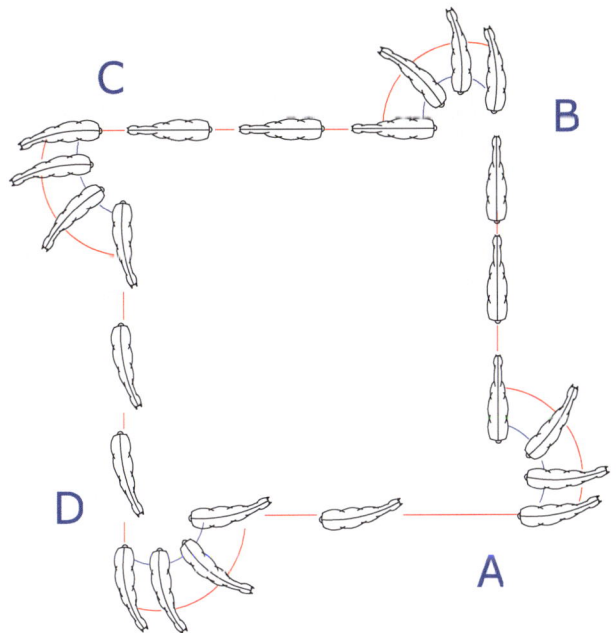

Figure 13-1

As you and your horse progress you will probably find yourself doing a credible shoulder-in during the *move out* phase of the exercise. However, it's best not to worry about the details of a shoulder-in at this stage — just do a few lateral steps to the next corner. The goal for now is only to have the horse do the exercise easily in response to light, relaxed cognitive aids.

The Octagon

Once the horse is doing the *turn in, move out* on the square with ease, you can modify the exercise by changing it from a 4-sided square to an 8-sided octagon. As with the previous exercises the emphasis should be on the horse doing the exercise easily in response to light cognitive aids.

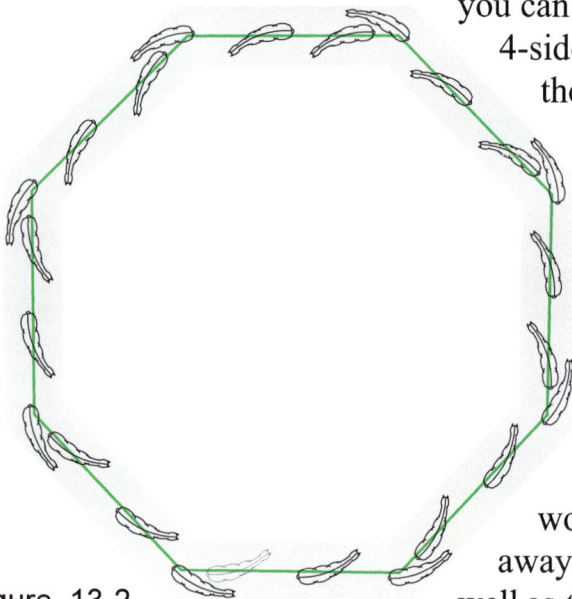

The 8 sides of the figure are created by asking your horse to *move out* for several strides, and then asking him to *turn in* for 2 or 3 strides.

It is very important that your horse is working off of cognitive aids and *moving out* away from your light touch of the inside leg, as well as *turning in* as a response to your outside rein and leg. If you mechanically turn him in by pulling his nose or move him out by pulling him over with the inside rein, you're wasting your time.

Figure 13-2

Finally a Circle

After you're able to easily do an 8-sided figure as shown above, it's a small matter (literally!) to change it to a 16-sided figure. As this drawing shows, when ridden on horseback a 16-sided figure is, for all practical purposes, a round circle.

The difference between riding the circle and the octagon is the frequency with which we change from *turn in* to *move out*. For the octagon there are several *move out* strides followed by 2 or 3 strides. For the circle it's a more sequential *turn in, move out, turn in, move out* cycle. As you and your horse become more practiced at this, you'll be asking him to *move out* and *turn in* within each stride, in such a subtle way that it will be more a matter of thinking it than doing it.

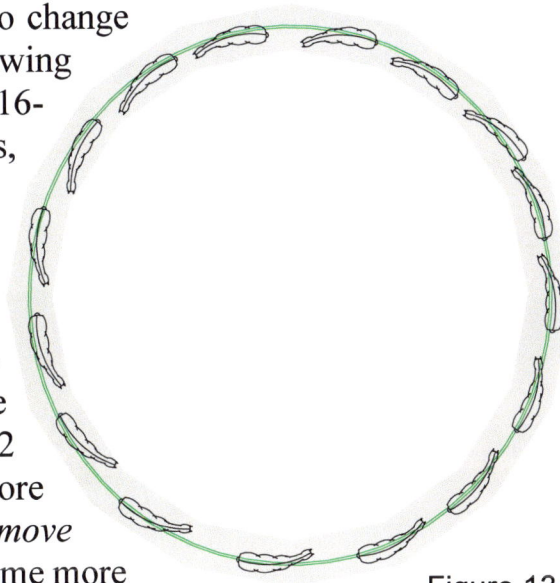

Figure 13 - 3

Fixing Circles

Once you're on a circle (Figure 13-4, A) there are three difficulties that can, and probably will, come up. Your horse can fall in (-B-), run out (-C-), or fall out (-D-).

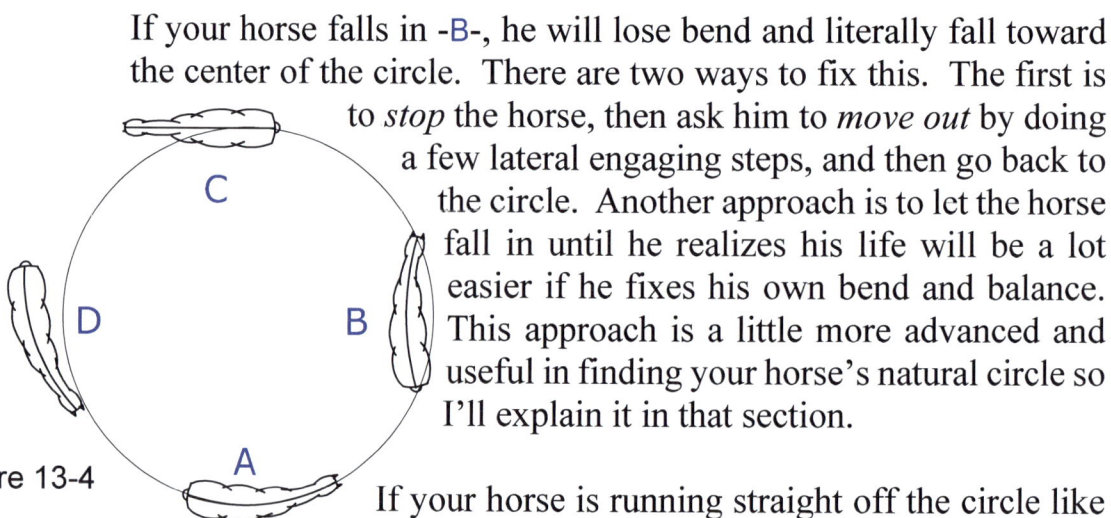

If your horse falls in -B-, he will lose bend and literally fall toward the center of the circle. There are two ways to fix this. The first is to *stop* the horse, then ask him to *move out* by doing a few lateral engaging steps, and then go back to the circle. Another approach is to let the horse fall in until he realizes his life will be a lot easier if he fixes his own bend and balance. This approach is a little more advanced and useful in finding your horse's natural circle so I'll explain it in that section.

C

D

B

A

Figure 13-4

If your horse is running straight off the circle like horse -C- in this diagram, he has lost his bend, is above the bit and bracing against you with the base of his neck. In this situation you only have one good option, and that is to *stop* him. It's very likely you'll have to *stop* him mechanically and somewhat abruptly when first dealing with this problem. Once he is stopped, release the aids before proceeding and give him a moment to settle. Then, use cognitive aids to turn him in to the circumference of the circle and *go* again. The greener the horse, the more you'll have to repeat this.

It's not at all unusual for a horse to give up running out at one point of the circle and then try another spot — as though looking for the invisible doorway that must be there someplace. However, after assuring himself there is no weak spot to burst through, most horses will relax and settle in to their fate. When they do, they *soften* their muscles, relax into their frame, and bend through their bodies. So, you very often fix an entire array of the most common problems encountered in training by simply insisting the horse *go* where you tell him to with light cognitive aids.

I say the above method — stopping, correcting, and beginning again — is the only "good" option because the alternative (and much more frequently suggested) approach is to use "more outside hand and leg" to hold him on the circle mechanically. The problem with this is that it teaches the rider to ride badly, with dull insensitive aids, instead of teaching the horse to be more sensitive to correct light aids. Although you may be strong enough to keep a horse on a figure that looks a bit like a circle with this method, horses ridden this way will remain against the hand and rigid in their bodies.

A horse that over bends to the inside and drifts out laterally is falling out (Figure 13-4, D). Horses do this when their "hollow" side is on the outside of the circle and the rider is trying to hold the horse's nose on the circle with the inside rein instead of keeping the horse's shoulder on the circle with the outside rein.

A horse is "hollow" on a side when he avoids rein contact on that side of his mouth. A horse that is hollow on one side will always be "stiff" on the other side. It's important to distinguish a horse falling out from a horse running straight through because using "more outside hand" is the wrong thing to do with a horse running through and the correct thing to do with a horse falling out.

The solution to fixing a hollow horse (also known as "one sidedness" — an actual word in dressage speak) as well as the falling out is to put the horse on the circle with the "hollow" side out. Then the rider has to make the contact even in both reins by taking up more on the outside and softening the contact on the inside. While this sounds simple enough, most horses tend to object disproportionately to this exercise. They throw their heads up, invert their bend, and try to run out or fall in. However, if you can stick with it for a few minutes, keep the contact even on both reins while ignoring the horse's frame and bend, most horses will soon settle. Then they figure out the easiest and most comfortable way to deal with even contact is to put their heads down, bend, and stretch into the outside rein. This exercise is best done on your horse's "natural circle".

The Natural Circle

For every horse at every gait, there is a circle of a certain size on which the horse will find it easiest to learn to balance a rider. When you ride your horse on this circle, you'll find it's very easy to regulate his speed, engage his hind legs, and get him to relax and bend his back while he stretches to, but not through, the outside aids. I call these circles "natural circles." The idea of riding a horse on a circle based upon his conformation is not a new idea — the classical "volte" was determined by a ratio of the length of the horse's back to the diameter of the circle.

A horse's natural circle is a circle just small enough that he has to move slightly laterally to stay on it. This puts him in a shallow shoulder-in or shoulder-fore position. If a circle is too small he won't be able to move freely. If the circle is too big, there is no incentive for him to move laterally and the rider is left with nothing but the reins to try to mechanically regulate speed, tempo, bend, and frame.

Figure 13-5 illustrates this. Horse -D- is on a circle so small he has to go around it almost perpendicular to the circumference — very close to the lateral engaging step exercise. This has the advantages of the lateral engaging step but it doesn't allow the horse to move freely forward. At the other extreme, horse -A- is on a circle so large he can go around and around on it for years and years (as so many horses have) without ever learning to bend and *soften* in his body.

Horse -B- would, at first glance, seem to be right on target. He's on a circle that he can bend to stay on. With a horse that has already learned how to bend, balance, and move into the aids, this is the ideal. However, with horses not yet this advanced, it is not as helpful as the circle horse -C- is on.

Figure 13 -5

Horse -C- is on his natural circle. To stay on this circle, horse -C- has to move at a slight angle. Simply riding on this circle helps to teach the horse how to bend and stretch into the outside aids.

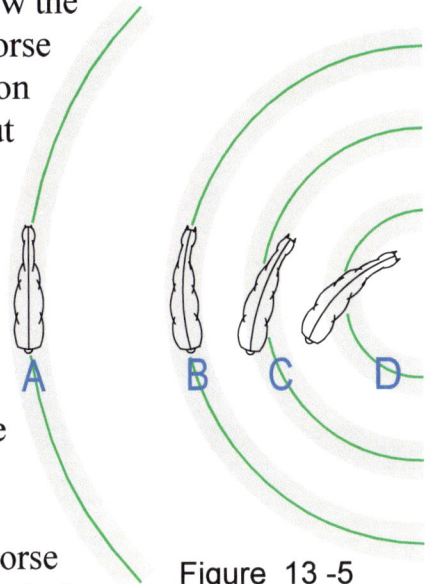

Finding the Natural Circle

A good way to find your horse's natural circle is to walk him in to a very small circle and keep him there until he begins to *soften*. Then give him a very light aid — a soft whisper of a cognitive aid — asking him to *move out* laterally. As soon as he responds by taking any outward step, drop the reins in reward and let him rest or a moment or two. Repeat this exercise until he begins to feel as though he wants to *move out* on his own as soon as you bring the circle in. When this happens, you can find your horse's natural circle by adjusting the diameter until your aids asking him to *turn in* are in balance with his asking for permission to *move out*. The dressage speak for this feeling is, "moving from your inside leg to your outside hand." When he is on this circle and you have this feeling, you will find it very easy, virtually effortless, to hold him on the circle you want.

Teaching your horse to begin moving out as you're turning him in may seem at odds with the previous exercises, which dealt with the horse running through and falling out. However, in those situations your horse was being stiff or hollow and going through the aids instead of into them. To do this exercise your horse must be working off cognitive aids to easily *turn in* and *move out*. If he isn't, he isn't yet ready for this so you need to go back to earlier exercises to make him more responsive to light aids.

As your horse begins to correctly move into the aids on the circle, he will become connected. When he is, you can spiral the circle in or out by just pointing your belly button to where you want to go. With a little practice you'll learn to keep your horse on connected aids all the time regardless of whether you're doing a volte or straight line. Furthermore, whenever your horse does begin to lose balance, you'll be able to restore it by doing a small circle — a volte. This is the beginning of using figures and movements to correct your horse instead of trying to fix him with "more hand" or "more leg."

Getting a simple circle right will give you and your horse the feeling of what a very well trained school horse is like. It is the basis of everything that is important in dressage, so it's well worth the effort. From this you will have the sensation of physically moving your horse from your inside leg to outside hand and leg. However, you're not physically pushing your horse into your outside aids — you're experiencing connection — the effortless conversation of two beings fluent in the same language.

Connected Contact

A major element of connection and connected riding is a particular type of contact. Generally contact is defined as any connection that goes from rider, through the reins to the horse. However, what I'm calling "connected contact" is different from the simple, just touching, contact of cognitive riding.

"Connected Contact" can be objectively defined as a contact the horse "stretches into." In other words, when a horse is going in a connected way, he will slightly lengthen his frame as he reaches over his top line and into the hand while maintaining his bend and tempo.

This bit of information is both definitive and diagnostic. If your horse isn't reaching into the bridle, you need to either increase or decrease the amount of contact you have in your hand. If you don't offer enough contact to the horse, there is nothing for him to reach into, so he won't. If your contact is too tight or rigid, you prevent the horse from reaching into the contact, so he can't.

The "connected contact" that falls between too little or too much is not a precise point that must be met exactly — it is a range of contact. You'll find there is a comfortable zone within which you can vary the contact yet retain your connection.

14 The Shoulder-In

*N*o book on dressage is complete without a chapter on the shoulder-in. However, there is very little to say about it in this book since we're using a bottom up, cognitive approach.

If you've been following the program you're already doing the movement. Just riding your horse on his natural circle is riding him in a shoulder-in on a circle. Since your horse's natural circle is a little too small for him to be able to bend to match its circumference — he has to move at a slight angle. When he's moving at that slight angle with an even bend, it's a shoulder-in.

Figure 14-1 shows the horse moving in a shoulder-in on his natural circle -A-. Going from a shoulder-in on a circle to a shoulder-in on a line is only a matter of spiraling out to a very big circle. You may recall from earlier that spiraling out to a larger circle is just a matter of doing a little more *move out* than *turn in*. Going back to the smaller circle is just a matter of more *turn in*. The horse in the figure simply *moved out* for a few strides on the line -B-. Then, before things could fall apart, he *turned in* to a circle again -C-.

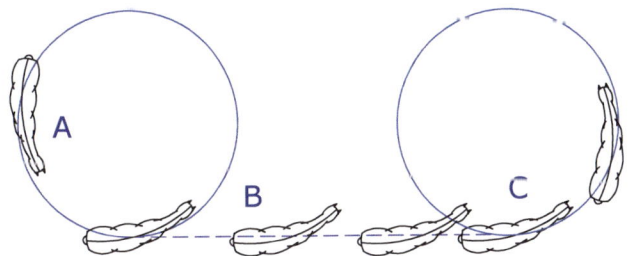

Figure 14-1

As you practice this you'll find it easy to stay on the line for more and more strides. It won't be long before you can just do a shoulder-in for as long as you want without any effort at all. Then it's a small matter to ride a shoulder-in wherever you want. Doing the movement from one dressage ring letter to another will be child's play.

For many readers, this explanation of how to do a shoulder-in seems short, simplistic, and lacking in detail. The reason it seems this way is that it's a "How to do a Shoulder-In" chapter that uses the bottom up, cognitive method and builds on the five basics. You and your horse already know how to do the basics. A shoulder-in is just a very slight adjustment.

This is also easier and shorter because we first teach the horse to do the movement and then, when he can do it easily, have him do it where you want it — usually this is from dressage letter to letter.

The long convoluted descriptions of the movement with complex explanations of the aids, are long and convoluted because they're top down and mechanical. They explain the shoulder-in as though it was something different and apart from the training that preceded it. Now you know, it is exactly the same as everything else in dressage. There is no need for different aids or a different approach to training and riding it.

15

Developing Corners

A defining idea of dressage is that it teaches a horse that the easiest, most comfortable way to carry his rider is by bending and stepping out to the corner or curve he is on. Ideally, a horse will corner very much like a train on a track bends on a curve. Like that train, the horse will be constantly bending or straightening as he goes through the corner.

In dressage, a corner is defined as one quarter of a small circle, yet in terms of training, it is almost the opposite of a circle. The circle is infinite while the corner is fixed and very limited. The circle can be done away from the walls of the arena, while the corner is defined by the walls of the arena.

We saw in a previous chapter that you can use the Natural Circle to give your horse the idea of bending and moving out while on a circle.

However, you can stay on a circle as long as you need to adjust your bend and get your horse moving out correctly. You can also work on a circle far enough from the walls of the arena that they have no effect. So, we need a different strategy for training corners.

Trying to mechanically hold and bend the horse on an ideal corner doesn't work very well. As in all mechanical riding, it teaches the horse to brace against the reins and lean on the rider. However, it's a simple matter to teach him to do a corner correctly if you give him the time to figure out what is expected, and then let him learn how to do it the right way.

Figure 15-1 shows three stages of training your horse to bend through corners. When first training corners begin by turning in from the track early, and then ask your horse to *move out* as you go through it until you're back on the track again.

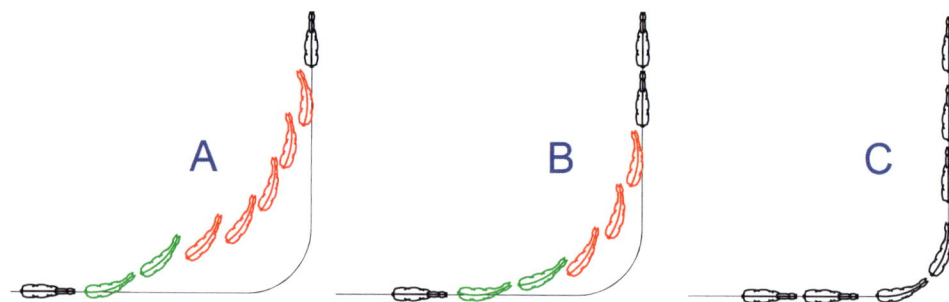

Figure 17-1

Section -A- in the diagram shows this earliest stage. The horse drawn in black is on the ideal track. The horse in green is turning-in from the track a good distance from the corner. By having the horse *turn in* this early the rider can encourage him to bend as he asks him to *move out* to the ideal line again. The horse moving out is in red. Finally, the horse back on the ideal track is drawn in black.

As the horse begins to learn how to bend through corners this way, you'll be able to stay closer to the ideal track as you ride through the corner. Section -B- shows the horse turning in closer to the ideal corner and moving out to the ideal track sooner. Within a few weeks your horse should learn to bend as he enters the corner and straighten as he leaves it as shown in section -C- above .

Taking the time to teach your horse to corner correctly has tremendous advantages as every correctly ridden corner helps to keep your horse supple and engaged. So, you come out of every corner with a well balanced horse ready to perform the next movement. Furthermore, a horse that is used to going through corners correctly will virtually half-halt himself as he approaches each corner as he will be anticipating his need to stay balanced through it.

This technique of turning in a little early and moving out to the perfect line is useful for training in general, and essential when riding in the competition ring.

16

The Half-Halt

*M*y definition of a half-halt is:

> ... a collecting exercise in which the hind legs become more engaged, shifting slightly more weight onto the horse's quarters, lightening forehand, and increasing attention. The half-halt is used in preparation for changes of movement, transitions, and whenever improved balance is required. The aid for the half-halt is a hardly visible, almost simultaneous, coordinated action of the rider's seat, legs, and hands.

I use my definition because it correctly explains the half-halt as something the horse does. The FEI and USEF definition of a half-halt says it's something the rider does. They claim it's:

"a hardly visible, almost simultaneous, coordinated action of the seat, the legs and the hand of the rider..."

My definition is right — their definition is wrong! They should change their definition because it's the source of a great deal of misunderstanding, and is responsible for a lot of backwards, mechanical, forceful riding.

The very suggestion that a "simultaneous, coordinated action of the seat, the legs and the hand of the rider" in any way engages and re-balances the horse is the epitome of the top down, mechanical language of dressage. Within this rule, the sanctioning bodies of dressage actually state you should sit up, push, and pull at the same time to engage and collect your horse[1]. As a result, thousands if not millions of riders actually think they're supposed to simultaneously push and pull, and thousands if not millions of horses learn to brace against the hand as they try to move forward against a stiff, resistant rider. Is it any wonder that mechanical riding has become an issue at horse competitions world-wide?

... it's not because you sit up that the horse sits down!

To be sure, if you sit up on a fully trained horse as you tickle the reins and touch with your legs, he will very definitely step under, engage, and collect. However, it is not because you sit up that the horse sits down! It is because the horse went through a cognitive, bottom up training program that taught him to respond this way and physically conditioned him to be able to do so.

The good news is that teaching a horse to half-halt correctly is one of the easiest things to do — if you begin the process as a cognitive

---

[1] DR108 The Half-Halt.

The half-halt is a hardly visible, almost simultaneous, coordinated action of the seat, the legs and the hand of the rider, with the object of increasing the attention and balance of the horse before the execution of several movements or transitions between gaits or paces. In shifting slightly more weight onto the horse's quarters, the engagement of the hind legs and the balance on the haunches are facilitated for the benefit of the lightness of the forehand and the horse's balance as a whole.

"half-*stop*" and then, over time, let it develop into a connected half-halt.

However, before you can think about doing a half-*stop*, your horse has to be doing good stops. You have to be able to gently ask your walking horse to *stop* with cognitive aids. There should either be no change in contact, or even a slight lessening of it. There are just a few incremental steps to build on the *stop* basic in order to make it a half-*stop*. Begin by walking along, then ask your horse to *stop*. As soon as he does *stop*, ask him to *soften* by first giving the reins for a moment, and then gently raising one or the other. Do it so the effect is similar to the flexions you have already done from the ground. In short hand, the procedure is:

go, stop, soften.

If you repeat this for a while, your horse will begin to anticipate the *soften* that you'll ask for as soon as he stops. Then, he'll begin to *soften* as you're stopping. The the procedure will then be:

go, soften, stop.

The horse will *soften* in anticipation of stopping because he's learned that it's easier to *stop* when he is soft than when he is stiff. Your role as trainer in this process is to keep your aids cognitive and as unobtrusive as possible while you let the exercise train the horse.

The next incremental step is to do a "half-*stop*." Do a half-*stop* by walking along, and then asking your horse to *stop*. As he does begin to *stop*, change your mind. Simply say to him with your aids, "Ya know what? I think maybe we should keep going." I'm not being flip by describing the aids this way, they really should be this conversational and nonchalant.

If your horse picks up on your decision to keep going, give him a little pat, and keep going. After you've walked long enough that he won't be confused, asking him to "half-*stop*" again, ask again. "Long enough that he won't be confused" is probably half or three quarters of a circle, or perhaps halfway down the long side of your arena.

I really do want the aids to be this nonchalant.

If your horse actually stopped when you asked for your half-*stop* don't worry about it and don't get aggressive. Simply release for a short moment and then ask him to move on again. Perhaps the next time you'll ask for the *stop* more gently or suggest he keep going a bit sooner, but don't try to fix it with stronger more aggressive aids.

Eventually, the difference between your horse "half-stopping" and coming to a complete *stop* will become more a difference of what you think than what you consciously do. Somewhere in that process, your horse will figure out it's easier to step under so he is ready for either. When he does — it's a half-halt.

Well, I told you it was easy.

Later you can do the same thing going from trot to walk. Teach canter half-halts with transitions from canter to walk or halt. Teaching canter half-halts with transitions to the trot is tricky because green horses tend to fall into the trot and go rushing off. So I don't advise it.

17 Change Through the Circle

*T*his simple figure is an excellent demonstration of the five basics working together. As you practice it you'll find your horse becoming more skilled at each of the basics, and more fluid in his ability to go from one basic to the next.

Begin work on this figure fairly early on. Don't wait until each of the basics is perfected as this is the type of exercise that will help to perfect them. When working on it, you don't have to constantly change direction as though you are on a figure eight. Stay on the circle for a bit, and when you're ready, change direction through the circle. Then, circle the other way until you're ready to change again.

In coming chapters, I'll explain how to use the change through the circle as a basis for many of the remaining figures and movements in dressage. I do this to emphasize the continuity of the training process. You don't stop working on one thing and then begin working on something else. Everything builds on earlier work and relies on everything else in training.

You'll know your horse is laterally supple and ready move on with more advanced work when he easily changes through the circle in both directions. By "easily" I mean "effortlessly." Your horse should be on the aids and connected, reaching softly out to the bit as he bends to match the curve he is on.

While working on this and the other figures and exercises, try to relax and allow your aids to be second nature. Yes, you may think, "*turn in* here," but see what happens if you don't "try" to turn your horse or even worry about how you ask him to turn. Simply think it and let your aids act on their own as your horse turns in. This is very much the way it would be if you were walking on the ground and decided you wanted to turn. You would turn without giving any conscious thought whatsoever as to how to do it.

If you think "*turn in* here" but your horse doesn't do it, then gently *stop* him, turn him in with a step or two of schooling turn, and try the figure again. If your horse doesn't improve with this approach, you have to abandon the figure or movement for a while. Then, work only on the *turn in* basic until your horse does it when you think it before returning to the original exercise.

I have found the best size of circle to change through will typically be somewhere between 12 and 18 meters in diameter. This is a little more than half to a little less than the full width of a dressage arena. The way to know which circle is correct for your horse is to try it at different sizes until you find the circle that is easiest to work on. However, don't get locked into this — you'll find this size changes as you vary the exercises and your training progresses.

With that understood, we can take a quick look at the change through the circle shown in Figure 17-1. Start by turning in at -A-. As you approach the center, release and then change the bend at -B-. Then *move out* into your new bend -C- until you're back on the circumference -D-, and your change through the circle is complete.

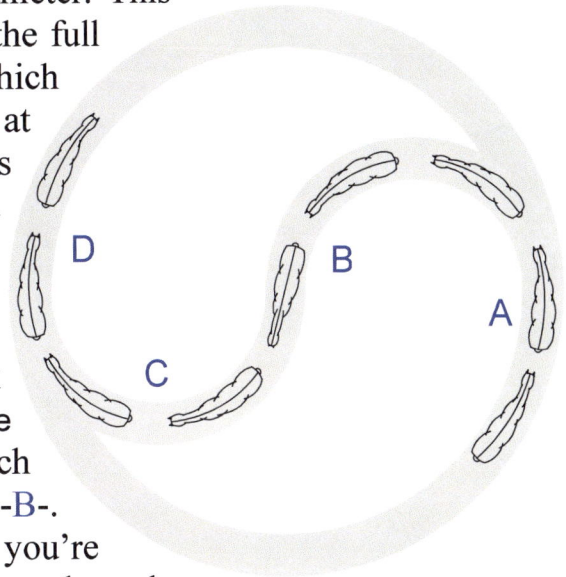

Figure 17-1

Release of Bend and Change of Weight

In the above paragraph I mentioned you should release and then change the bend at -B-. This is not as simple as it appears — at least not for the horse. When traveling on a curve, we want dressage horses to bend to match the curve they're on and stay upright. Left to his own devices, a horse will bend in the opposite direction of the curve he's on and lean in, using his head and neck as a counter balance. So, teaching your horse to move in a way that is totally opposite his nature is quite an accomplishment.

From his work on the natural circle, your horse should already understand how to bend, stretch, and reach out to the outside aids in both directions. He hasn't, however, had practice changing his bend and moving from one outside hand to the other. So we have

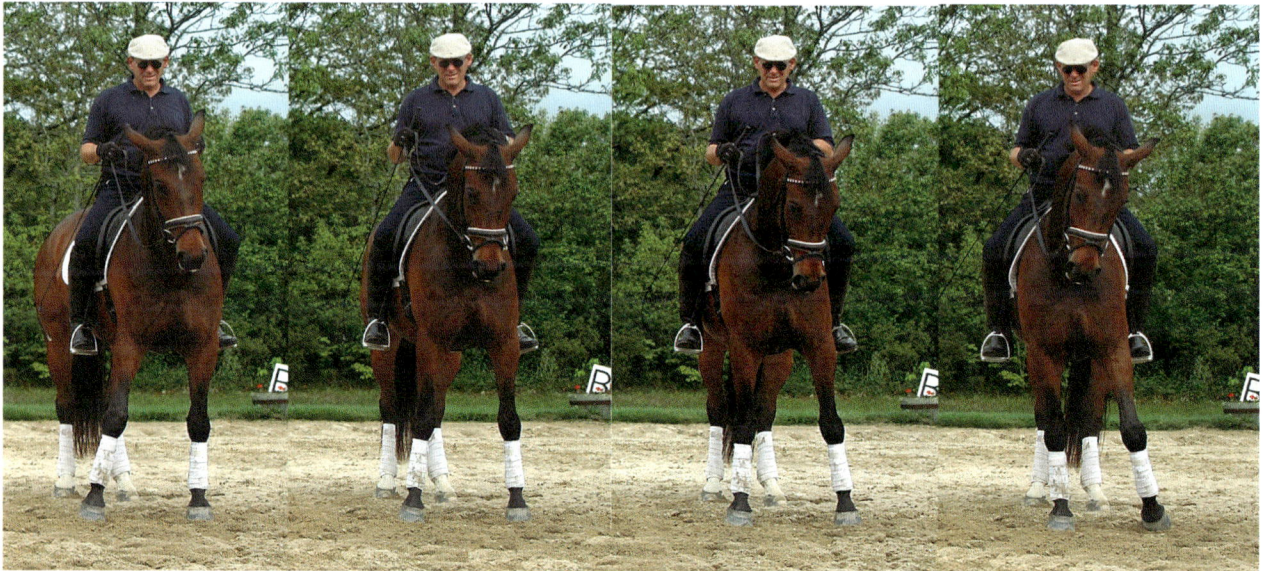

| Figure 17-2 | Figure 17-3 | Figure 17-4 | Figure 17-5 |

to go through a training process to teach the horse how to change his bend and shift his weight to stay upright. Begin by building on the skills the horse learned in the lateral engaging step.

The simplest and easiest way I can think of to teach this is by walking on a circle and then turning in to change through the circle. As you approach the point where you want to change bend, come to a *stop*. Release the aids for a moment, and then shift your horse's weight and change his bend by asking him to *move out* from your new inside leg. As he changes bend, begin to *move out* to the circle again. Once on the circle in the new direction, reward with either a pat on the neck or a quick break. When you're ready, change bend in the other direction.

The change of bend would look very much like Figures 10, 9-12 from Chapter 10 *Move Out* which I've shown again here as Figures 17, 2-5.

These pictures show a horse shifting his weight as part of changing his bend while standing in one place without moving his feet.

The horse on the left (Figure 17-2) is just finishing his last lateral engaging step away from my right leg. In the next frame (Figure 17-3) he has straightened and is balancing evenly on all four legs. (Figure 17-4) shows him shifting his weight to his right, so that he can change his bend in anticipation of moving away from my left leg (Figure 17-5). (Notice the straightened, shifted his weight, and bent in the opposite direction in these pictures without moving his feet at all.)

As you begin the exercise of changing through the circle, allow the horse to *stop* while re-balancing if necessary. It won't take long for him to only have to almost *stop* instead of coming to a full *stop* to change this way. Once he's able to almost *stop* to change bend and direction, he'll realize it's easier to do it this way than by fully stopping.

Almost stopping to change bend creates an additional factor to be considered. As horses change bend, they lengthen their frame slightly in the process. Green horses in longer frames more so than advanced horses in collected frames, but they all have to lengthen to a degree. When you were coming to a complete *stop*, you released the aids which allowed him to lengthen as well as re-balance.   Now that you're almost stopping, you can't completely release the aids. So in order to allow your horse to lengthen as he goes forward into the new bend, you have to "release" the old bend.

The aids to change through the circle with a release of bend are: *turn in* from the circle. As you approach the center, *soften* the outside rein just enough that the horse will lengthen as he reaches into the contact. As he reaches out to the contact he will begin to straighten, which will begin to shift his weight from the outside to towards the center. As he straightens, ask him to *move out* in the other direction by bringing your new inside leg (your right leg in the drawing) forward. You may also find it helpful to bring your new inside (right) hand slightly up and forward as you ask him to *move out* to the left.

As you can see from the Figure 17-1, as the horse is changing bend there is a moment of straightness when he is between the bends. I'll talk more about that later, but note there a point where he is physically straight and his weight is even on left and right.

As you continue to ask the horse to *move out* in the new direction he'll continue to adjust his bend accordingly. As he does you want to "catch" him in your new outside aids. Then, just follow his new bend back out to the circle.

"Oh my gosh!" you're thinking, "all that just for a change through the circle?"

Yes, and a little more, but don't panic yet. You don't have to do this like the perfectly shaped drawing on this page. In fact, your early attempts will probably look more like funny shaped oval things with squiggly lines in the middle. It doesn't make any difference how imperfect your early attempts are. It is much more important that you and your horse remain loose and relaxed than your figure look anything at all like it will later in training. So take as much time and space as your horse needs to shift his weight and change his bend. As it becomes easier and easier for both of you to do, you will find your figure looks more and more like this drawing.

Now — for that "little more" part...

Lateral Elevation

When a horse shifts his weight from side to side, his withers travel in a very slight upward arc, the highest point being in the moment of straightness. You can feel this in your hips on the ground very easily.

Stand with your legs slightly apart and your knees straight. Put most of your weight on your right leg and then shift your weight to your left leg. Shift your weight back and forth this way and you should feel a very tiny lightness and elevation in your hips as you pass your moment of straightness — the point where you have equal weight on both feet.

This little feeling of lightness and elevation is the reason I said when your horse is changing bend, you want to "catch" him in your new outside aids. When changing bend and direction, you really do want to feel as though you are gently tossing your horse from hand to hand and leg to leg as though he was a child's toy ball. Effortless, floating, easy. This feeling won't come to you right away, but when it does you'll know what it is.

Being aware of these facts and feelings is a good thing. It will make you a much better rider when you feel them on your horse. Like a few grains of salt on a meal, they will enhance your training technique and your horse's performance.

However, these few grains of salt cannot replace correct longitudinal elevation that can only come from proper collection. Every now and then you see a horse that's been trained to a fairly high level of performance with lateral elevation. Invariably these horses cross their legs in the piaffe and throw themselves from side to side in the changes. I mention this so you won't fall into that trap.

Extending the Moment
of Straightness

At some point, hopefully in the not too distant future, you will be able to walk and trot the change through the circle in both directions, tossing your horse from hand to hand, with relative ease. At that point, you want to interrupt that toss right in the moment of straightness and capitalize on it for a few strides.

Exactly how this is done is another of those things you have to feel your way with. You might try asking your horse to move into the new bend more gently as you catch him with your new outside aids a moment sooner. It's probably a good idea to do this at the walk a few times so you both have an easier time of figuring it out.

When you do get it, your horse will be physically straight and just a tiny bit elevated at his wither. Balance him there for a few moments or strides. Before he falls apart, which may only be in two or three strides at the beginning, softly finish the change of bend by asking him to *move out* some more. Then follow the new bend onto a circle in the new direction.

As time goes on you'll be able to keep him straight for more strides, and still be able to finish by gently moving him out to the new bend and continuing on. Eventually you'll be able to come out of a corner, go across the diagonal with a straight and slightly elevated horse, move him into the new bend as you approach the end of the diagonal, and never once have your horse fall on his forehand.

The only magic to this has been the cognitive, bottom up training method. We started slowly with a small figure. As he developed balance and strength, we gradually increased his energy and the size of the figure. In this way, he always stayed calm and balanced.

I think this method compares favorably to riding "forward" across the diagonal on an unbalanced, untrained horse. With that approach, pulling on the reins is the only tool you have to slow him down and bend him at the far corner. I've never had much luck with it.

18

Rein Back

*I*n its simplest form, the rein back is just the horse backing up. A well trained horse will rein back because he is soft and yielding to the rein. When he does, the reinback is a movement that relies on the horse's desire to move forward.

Visualizing a rein back as being "forward" is easy to do if you consider that an extended trot, a collected trot, and passage are all forward. Piaffe, which does not move forward at all, or very little, is still forward. The leap in logic of going forward from a piaffe to a rein back is not huge.

A forward-going rein back is a balance of *go, soften, and stop*. The rider asks the horse to *go* into a soft hand that says "no further." If the horse is *soft* through his body the energy becomes so collected it is a rein back in which the horse's balance remains uphill and he stays relaxed and supple. Going from a forward, relaxed, soft rein back to any other gait is a tiny matter of less *stop* as there is already enough *go*.

A rein back can be a backward movement if the horse braces against the rein instead of softening into it. When a horse is backing up by stiffening and bracing against the rein, he cannot transition smoothly from backward to forward. In order to change gears on a horse like that, you have to *stop* long enough for the horse to adjust his balance before he is physically capable changing direction from backward to forward.

Many dressage tests require the horse to rein back some number of steps and then proceed immediately in collected trot or canter. The point of the immediate transition after the rein back is to see that the horse is reining back as a result of his softening into the aids in balance, rather than because he is being pulled backward.

Aids

My preference is to sit slightly forward while asking the horse to *go* and gently preventing him from going with my *stop* aid. Plenty of good trainers will say, "No - you must sit back more while asking for the rein back!" Others will say you must sit straight.

The aid you choose doesn't matter as long as you make it consistent with your aids for extension and collection. For example, if your choice of aid for extension is to sit back a little more, and you sit a little less back for collection, then sit a little forward for rein back. If you choose to adjust your seat differently or not at all for collection and extension, be consistent as you go to rein back.

Development

There are many methods and approaches to teaching a horse to rein back. I'm offering this approach as an example because it is easily described with the tools and basics explained in this book. I begin at the walk and then ask the horse to *stop*. Then I release for a moment and follow that by asking for a rein back with a big cognitive aid.

My big cognitive aid for teaching the rein back consists of asking the horse to *go*, while sitting forward and raising my hands to cognitively *stop* the horse. Most horses will initially hesitate as if to say, "Huh?" when I do this. I'll reward that hesitation by dropping the reins, and giving him a pat. The next few times I ask, I'll reward the hesitation again. Then I might ask him to hesitate longer or even rock back slightly without moving his feet at all. Whatever change I ask for, it will be tiny.

As time goes on — and it may be quite a bit of time, maybe weeks — I'll ask for more incremental improvements. Perhaps I'll reward him for just lifting a foot in anticipation of moving. Then it may become moving one foot back, then half of a step back, and then one step back. Eventually he will understand the concept of the rein back and my big cognitive aid for it.

At that point I want to make sure he is softening as he reins back. This is simply a matter of asking him to *soften*, then asking him to rein back, and then rewarding. Soon he'll realize it's easier to reinback when he is soft. When he does, he'll *soften* on his own in the movement. Then it's a question of asking him with more and more refined aids until they are invisible.

19 Developing the Half-Pass

"Bend your horse around your inside leg is as pure a mechanical statement as was ever made.

*T*he half-pass is a lateral movement in which the horse is bent evenly in the direction he is moving. He moves laterally by crossing his outside legs in front of his inside legs. The conventional description of the aids is to, "bend your horse around your inside leg while moving him forward and away from your outside leg."

As I mentioned at the start of this book, this description of the movement and aids are what I was working with the first time I sat on a fully trained school master. Having read about the half-pass and the aids for it, I was able to ride it on a finished horse. So my experience with this movement was top down — I rode the end result first.

However, that is not the experience horses have with half-pass. They don't start with the image of a finished movement and then try to do it. To teach a horse the half-pass, or any other movement, you have to start with something that's easy and familiar to him. Once he has that initial concept, you gradually increase the precision of the movement you are training. If you always keep your horse comfortable with the process he will eventually understand the finished "half-pass" as a concept. Then, he'll perform them easily and happily for you.

The idea, that the half-pass has to be cognitively trained from the bottom up, is completely missing from the conventional description of how to ride one. "Bend your horse around your inside leg while moving him forward and away from your outside leg," is as pure a top-down, mechanical statement as was ever made!

... the half-pass is just a schooling turn that moves forward.

Every half-pass has to be cognitively trained because our legs have no mechanical effect. So, the only way to teach a horse to bend or move from our legs is by cognitive means. We achieve this with the first tier basics *move out* and *turn in*. When the horse does these and the other basics in a connected way, you can put them together into more advanced movements and figures.

Viewed in terms of the five basics, the half-pass is just a schooling turn that moves forward. At least, that's the theory. We humans can immediately envision it as big forward moving *turn in* because we can learn from the top down. However, the horse has to be brought gradually around to this idea. He is also going to need to practice this for a while to develop the strength, coordination, and balance required for the exercise.

This movement is an example of training cognitively while the horse remains connected. He has to be connected and "on the aids" because he has to stay bent and reaching in order for it to be a half-pass. Yet, even though he's connected, we have to get him to understand what is wanted.

Figure 19-1 shows an early half-pass exercise. The figure includes the path of the change through the circle to show this is more a modification of that exercise than something new or separate from what we have been doing.

I always introduce this exercise by doing changes through the circle. Then when things are going well, I just stretch the figure out with a few steps of half-pass. With this form of the exercise it's pretty normal to start off with the haunches leading a little. Later, we'll be able to fix that.

Set up the half-pass by *moving out* a little -A- to increase the bend and put the horse in a very slight haunches-in position. Then, while keeping the Slight haunches-in position, come in off the track using a large schooling turn -B-. As you come around, simply increase your *go* and you'll do a few steps of half-pass -C-. When your horse begins to lose his bend - D-, don't argue with him or try to keep the half-pass mechanically. Just change bend normally as though it was your idea in the first place and *move out* to another circle -E-.

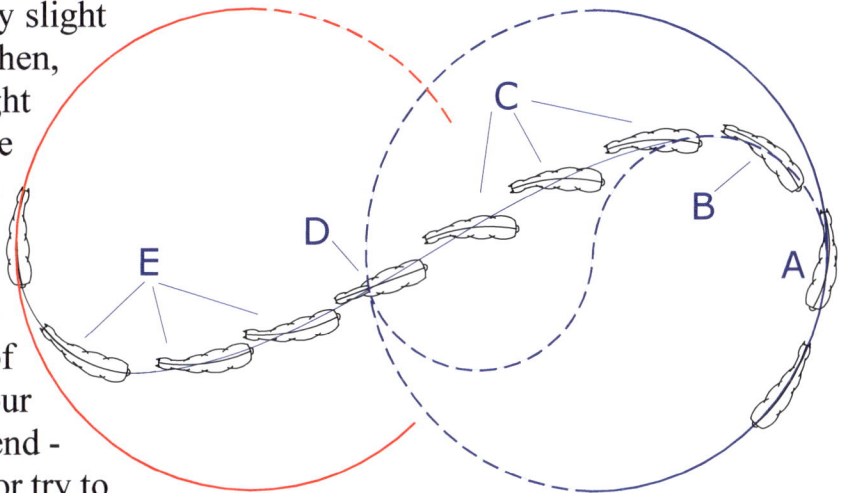

Figure 19-1

It doesn't matter that your horse may have only done two or three strides of half-pass like movement with very little crossing. It doesn't matter if his haunches were leading or trailing a little bit. Do a little of this exercise with him every day and over time you'll both find it easier and easier to continue for more strides at more of an angle with more crossing. The only trick is to keep it easy.

If you try to do the exercise mechanically you're lost since there is no way to force a half-pass.

There are many other ways of approaching the half-pass. Every one can be understood in terms of the five basics and each will be far more successful if your horse is proficient in those basics. I prefer this method because it offers a lot of flexibility. It can be modified by changing the size of the circle leading into the exercise. You can change the angle of the diagonal and the length of it.   It's reasonable to play with your horse's angle on the diagonal — you might have him correct, or he might go better with his quarters leading or trailing. Some horses will pick this up better at the walk, some at the trot, and some find it easier to do in the canter. This is simply a starting point — an introduction to the idea of half-pass. Precision is not an issue — making it easy and pleasant for your horse is.

Another approach is to have the horse do a shoulder-in on a very slight angle.   I show this exercise relative to the change through the circle to again emphasize that this should be done as a continuation of previous work. The exercise is as simple as can be. Come in from whatever circle you were on, do a few steps of shoulder- in and *move out* to a circle again.

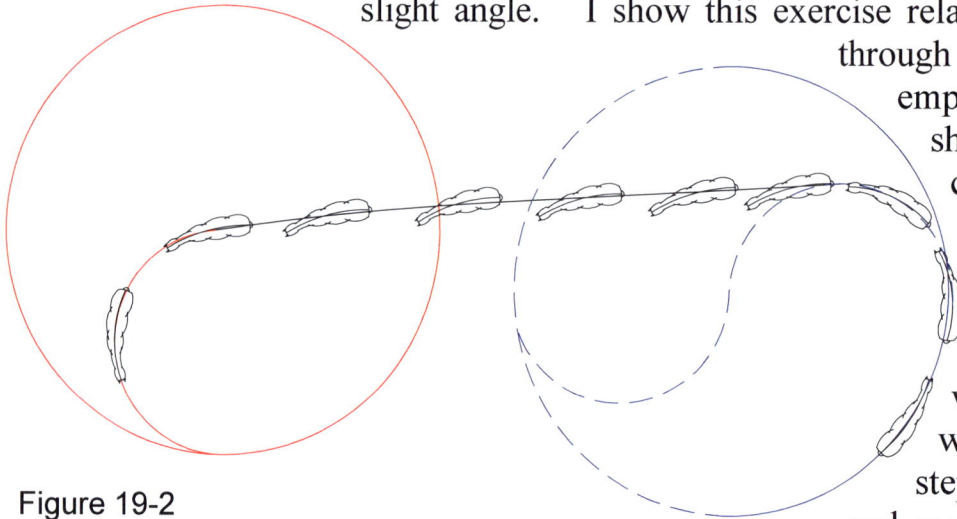

Figure 19-2

The interesting thing about this exercise is that the result is completely dependent on the angle of the line you ride. If it is within a certain range, your horse will do a baby half-pass. A little less or more angle, and your horse will simply do a shoulder-in.

This figure puts the angle in the perspective of a dressage ring. If you were to turn onto the centerline at the letter "A" in a standard dressage arena, you would want to be aiming for a point just a few meters to the left or right of the letter "C". There's no need to go that distance, just ride in that direction.

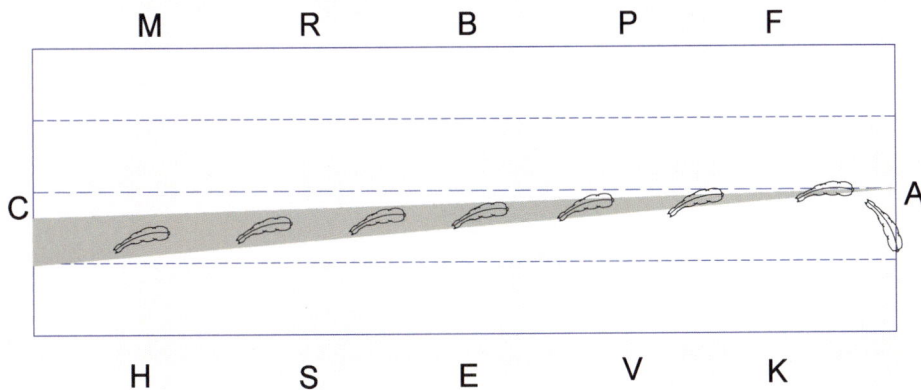

Figure 19-3

If you try to ride a shoulder-in on an angle that falls within that range your horse will bring his outside legs in front of his inside legs as he travels. This is the basic idea of the half-pass. However, if you ask for a shoulder-in on a line with less angle, or more of an angle, he'll simply do a shoulder-in on that line. I know this sounds a little crazy and doesn't seem like it should work, but it has worked with most horses I've tried it on.

Another very useful application of this is in an exercise called the "staircase." In the staircase exercise the horse is asked to do a few steps of half-pass followed by a few steps of shoulder-in. The point of the exercise is to reestablish the bend when the horse starts to lose it. So, in the exercise shown in Figure 19-1, at point -D-when the horse begins to lose his bend, you would do a few steps of shoulder-in to reestablish it, and then be able to continue on.

In the typical staircase exercise, the half-pass steps are done on a diagonal and the shoulder-in steps are done parallel to the long side. However, the exercise is easier to do and works better if you do the shoulder-in steps at the same shallow angle as shown in the above exercise.

Using these little exercises, your horse will soon have the concept of the half-pass. When he does, you can ride it with precision from letter to letter. Then, you will be able to ride through a corner of the ring onto the long side, half-pass out to X. There you can change the bend, and half-pass back to the long side in time to change bend once more and ride through the next corner. All this and not a single word about the five basics!

The five basics are now hidden but not gone — and they cannot be forgotten as we need them to correct problems as they occur. For instance, let's say you *go* through a corner just fine, ask for a half-pass and your horse continues down the long side. What do you do?

If you try twisting your body, or using more hand, leg, or seat than is comfortable to fix the half-pass, than your horse will be teaching you to ride badly rather than you teaching your horse to *go* properly. So the correct solution is to deconstruct the problem and figure out which basic isn't working, then fix that. The half-pass is just a big schooling turn with *go*, so if your horse is only going and not *turning in* when you ask for it, you have to go back and work on the *turn in* basic — then go back to the half-pass. Correcting the underlying basic at the core of the problem is the way successful trainers train.

20 The Flying Change

*T*he flying change is a fun, functional, and totally natural movement — horses do them in the fields all the time.

At its core, the flying change is a transition from a canter on one lead to a canter on the other. So my aid for a flying change is exactly the same as my aid for a transition to canter from any other gait. My primary considerations for good canter transitions are that the horse remains soft and balanced. By "soft" I mean that the contact remains the same or softer during the transition as he continues to stretch into my hand. By "balanced" I mean he should lift his wither and move into my outside aids as he does the transition. Said in the negative, he should not pull on me, fall on his forehand, or fall in. I achieve my goals and prevent these problems by having the horse *soften* and *move out* slightly in preparation for the canter. Then I slide my outside leg back a little as I sit up and think "canter".

You're ready to start flying changes when your horse does good transitions from walk to canter and canter to walk. You'll also need to be able to lengthen and shorten the stride as well as ride the canter straight, in shoulder-in, and haunches in positions.

I break the process of training changes into three phases. In the first phase, I just want to give the horse the idea of doing a change under saddle. With some horses this phase can be over in a few minutes or days. With others, it could take a few weeks. The key elements of this phase are preparation and compromise. By this I mean I don't worry about where or when I ask for the change,

I'm going to spend the time necessary to prepare him and when it feels right I'll ask for it. I'm also going to compromise a great deal on the quality of the change at this point — in fact, it doesn't even have to be a clean change. Any good effort will be rewarded.

There's a fairly clear line between phase 1 and 2 and you'll know you've crossed it when your horse begins to volunteer the change. It's totally normal for horses to decide changes are great fun once they've started to figure them out. Then, they want to do them all the time whether or not you've asked for it. So, in phase two my emphasis is on making the horse wait for me to ask him to change. I'm still not concerned with having him perform the change at a particular point — I'll ask for a change wherever I feel it's correct.

For instance, if I come across the diagonal and I feel my horse anticipating the change but waiting for my permission for a few strides, I'll ask for the change and then reward regardless of exactly where I am on the diagonal. As his training progresses I'll ask him to wait for my permission for longer and longer periods until eventually he just waits for my permission to change.

On the other hand, if my horse changes as soon as I turn onto the diagonal or at any time before I've asked for the change, then I'll immediately *stop* and pick up the original lead again. The only challenge here is to tell him he has to wait for me in a tactful enough way that I don't discourage him from changing altogether.

In phase three I'm less inclined to compromise and want to work on perfecting everything. The line between phase 2 and 3 is a little blurry, but when the horse is consistently waiting for you to ask him to change, and doing clean changes, you're there. Begin to look for each change to be done perfectly — perfect tempo, stride, straightness and softness.

When he can consistently do good changes like this, you can begin to do changes from one lead to another and then back again. At first, don't bother to even count strides between changes. Just do a change, get him settled and prepared for a change back, and then, change back. Later, a change every fourth stride, then every third. Much later, every second and then every stride.

Exercises

The first "flying change" exercise is the "simple change." This is another exercise I do as a "stretched out" change through the circle. The *turn in* to the first half- circle -A- helps to collect the canter in preparation for the transition to walk at -B -. The exercise "stretches out" as you take the time and space to do a good change of bend at the walk -C- that ends with your horse moving out — the correct preparation for the transition to canter at -D-. Continue moving the canter out for a few strides until you return to the larger circle -E-

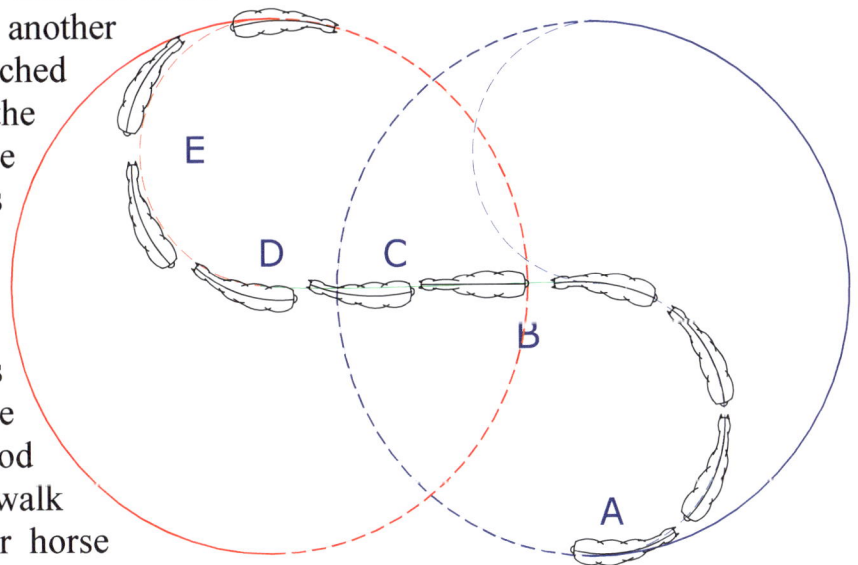

Figure 20-1

The emphasis on moving out is to prevent the horse from falling-in which is also falling on his forehand. So if your horse isn't perfectly straight or moving out a little, he's falling out of balance, and that is going to cause all sorts of problems down the road.

Second exercise in flying change.

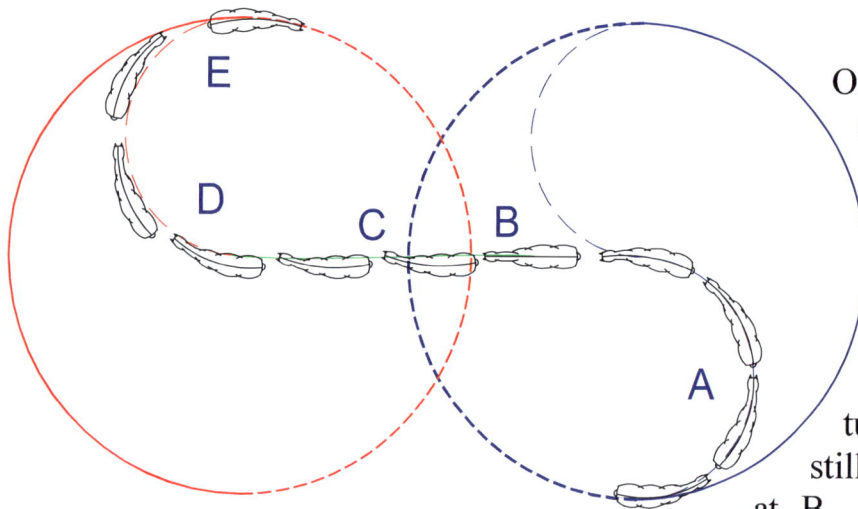

Figure 20-2

Once the horse has the simple change confirmed in both directions, modify that exercise to have him change bend in the canter and then walk. You see this in Figure 20-1 where the horse turns in at -A- and while still cantering, changes bend at -B-. At -C- he walks, then he picks up the canter at -D-. Last, he moves out to the large circle -E- just like in the first form of the simple change.

Over time eliminate the walk steps one by one — always being careful to keep a priority on moving out to the new canter. Done with some feeling, tact, and encouragement you'll soon find your horse doing an actual flying change.

Usually he'll learn to change in one direction before the other. In the other direction (or sometimes with some horses in both directions) you may find him not changing cleanly — he'll change in front but not in back, or he'll be a stride or two late in back. He may do what I call a "stutter step" that feels like half a stride of trot between one canter and the next. Whatever the symptom, it's not much of a problem — just the horse being a little clumsy while learning.

This is a good time to remember that dressage teaches horses the easiest most comfortable way to carry riders. This means we don't have to make them perform, we have to show them how to perform and then let them do it. So rather than trying to fix things by getting after the horse or throwing him into the change mechanically, solve problems by giving him some time to figure things out. You can also gently vary the preparation to help them as they're learning.

Part of the preparation for changes is getting the energy and length of stride just right. This is similar to approaching a jump and having just enough energy, tempo, and stride that the horse doesn't have to slow down or speed up to jump it. He literally takes it in stride.

If you think your horse may need more energy coming into the change you can modify the figure you're working on to give yourself more room to open up the horse's stride before the change. Figure 20-3 shows a

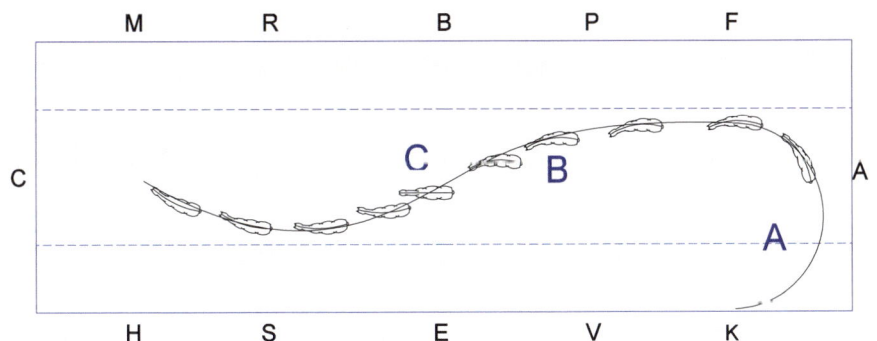

Figure 20-3

typical pattern in which you would *turn in* from the track -A-, do a little half-pass to engage the outside hind -B-, then change bend and do the flying change -C-.

If your horse has too much speed, try putting him on a 12-15 meter circle, and do canter/walk transitions every 3 to 4 strides. Using 3 to 4 strides between transitions is a terrific elevating and collecting exercise because a horse will do a correct upwards transition to the canter by coming up at the withers. In the same manner, he will elevate and collect to transition to walk from the canter.

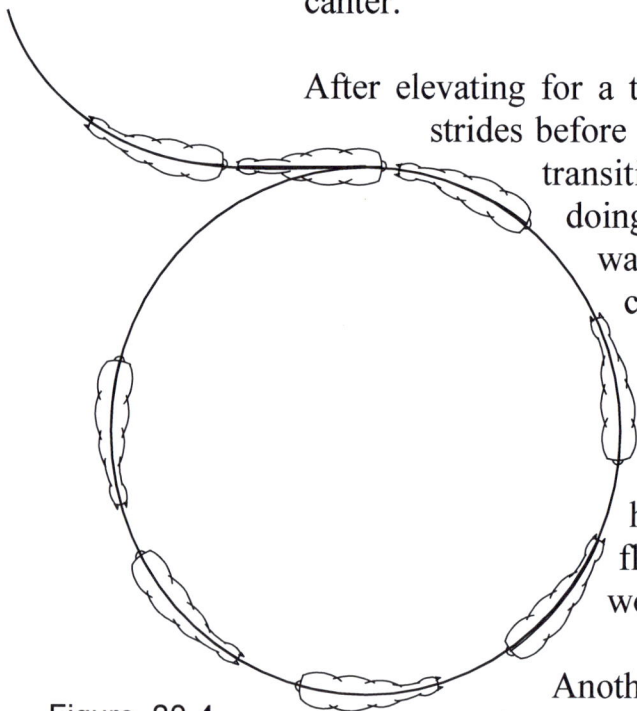

After elevating for a transition horses stay up for about three strides before starting to fall apart. So when you do a transition every three strides, they're always doing a nice elevated and collected canter or walk. (Over time, increase the number of collected strides and then you have a collected horse.) So if your horse has been too forward or fast for the changes, do the transitions on the circle and then, when it feels right, take up the canter just as you have, but then change bend and ask for a flying change. This figure shows what this would look like.

Figure 20-4

Another variable is straightness. In order to avoid having the horse lean or fall-in when doing changes, I advocate bending the horse for the new lead before the change. For instance, if I'm about to do a change from the left lead to the right, I like to have the horse already bent to the right before asking for the change. You can play with that bend — maybe a little more, maybe less. Some horses will have to be absolutely straight when learning. This is fine too since ultimately every horse should do changes absolutely straight.

You can also adjust the angle of the horse. Initially some horses find it easier to jump into the change from a little shoulder-in position, some from a haunches in position. It makes no difference — just figure out a way to get the horse changing — you can perfect it later.

Phases Two & Three

Once your horse has figured out the change, he is almost certainly going to start anticipating and trying to do them of his own volition. Very early on in the process, as your horse is just beginning to do changes, you may have to let him to get away with this a few times. However, after you allow a few like that, you have to start insisting that he wait for you to ask. This appears to be a horrible inconsistency — why allow your horse to change when he wants and then insist he wait to change only on your command?

This goes to the heart of cognitive training. I started with something that was easy for the horse, the change through the circle in the trot, then I made it a simple change of lead through the circle with canter - walk - canter transitions. Next I began to change the bend before the transition to walk, and then I started to eliminate the walk. Suddenly, he understands there is no walk! Now, he understands he going to change from one canter to the other!

This is an exciting moment for him. He thinks he has it all figured out — it's a flying change, something he has been doing all his life in the fields. On the other hand, you know he doesn't have it all figured out. You know there are lots of problems with his current version of a flying change. However, the fact that the change itself is flawed, perhaps horribly flawed, is not a concern to the cognitive trainer. The only thing that counts is the horse has the idea of a flying change. So, when you've let your horse do enough changes to confirm that idea, you move on to the next idea, which is that he should wait for you.

Waiting has to be the next priority. If your horse is not waiting for you to tell him what to do next, he's not responding to your *stop* or *soften* aids. He's bracing and pulling just like the horse bracing and running off the circle was when you were first putting the five basics together. As in that situation, your only option is to *stop,* release, re-balance, and try again. It is only after he has the ideas that he should remain *soft* and wait for you to ask before he does a flying change, that you can move on to phase three.

Phase three is the quest for perfection. It never ends. However, even though we're now working towards perfection, we're not insisting on it. If your horse is waiting do to his changes, but they're not straight enough, long enough, or precise enough, pick the worst of the lot and try to make it a little bit better over time. Let's say you think the worst thing about his changes is that he's not straight enough in them. Don't try to force him to be straight, try to get him to be less crooked. As his straightness gradually improves, you'll come to a point where it is no longer the worst thing about your changes.

Perhaps you'll decide that your horse has to change more precisely at the spot where you want - or "at the letter" to put this in dressage test terms. Again, don't try and force him to start doing the changes exactly at the spot you want, begin to work gradually towards always doing changes closer to the spot you choose.

If you're thinking, "Well, this strategy isn't just true of flying changes, it's the way to train everything!" then I have succeeded in gradually bringing you around to being a cognitive trainer who always keeps his horse calm, relaxed, and happy.

21 Counter-Canter

*T*HE COUNTER CANTER[1] is a movement in which the horse canters on the "wrong" lead at the request of the rider. For instance, while circling to the right, the horse would canter on his left lead. The counter-canter is unique in dressage because the horse is not bent to match the line he's on. In fact, he is not physically able to bend in the direction of movement while cantering this way.

The counter-canter is a considered a balance movement and it certainly has a balance component. However, since it is easier for a horse that knows how to do a flying change to change leads, than to stay on the counter lead, this a more a test of the horse's submission. It is also a good test of the rider's ability to train

---

[1] FEI Article 405-5. Counter-Canter

This is a movement where the rider, for instance on a circle to the left, deliberately makes his horse canter with the right canter lead (with the right fore leading). The counter-canter is a balancing movement. The horse maintains his natural flexion at the poll to the outside of the circle, and the horse is positioned to the side of the leading leg. His conformation does not permit his spine to be bent to the line of the circle. The rider, avoiding any contortion causing contraction and disorder, should especially endeavor to limit the deviation of the quarters to the outside of the circle, and restrict his demands according to the degree of suppleness of the horse.

cognitively since doing this movement requires the horse's understanding and willing compliance.

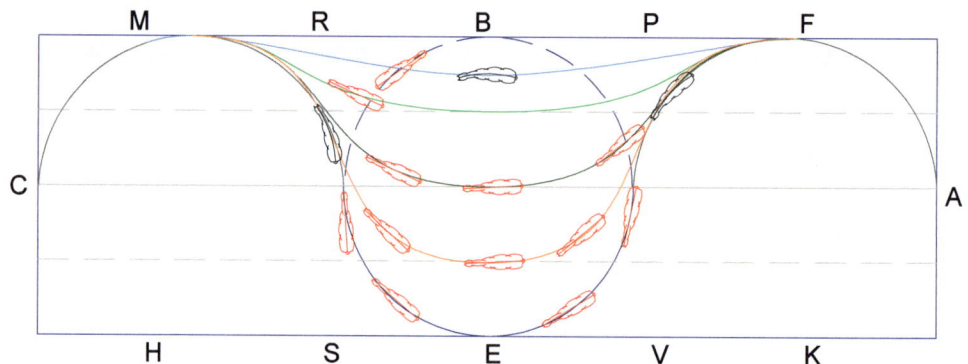

Figure 21-1

I introduce the counter-canter using the method shown in Figure 21-1. I start by riding in from the track just a bit, perhaps halfway to the quarter line, and then back to the track as shown by the green path. This is so easy for the horse that it really isn't quite counter-canter and requires no preparation. Once the horse is comfortable with that, I simply start to come in a little farther and farther from the track. You can see in the drawing that as the path gets further from the track, the part of the loop that is counter-canter (shown with red horses) becomes more curved and therefore more demanding for the horse.

If I take my time and keep it easy for the horse, I'll eventually have a three-loop serpentine. At that point I'm doing half of a 20 meter circle in counter-canter. I can then follow the second loop around to remain on the circle or to find myself back on the track, headed towards A in counter-canter.

This is not the only strategy for developing the counter-canter. It's simply another example of how training movements is always a matter of gradually introducing concepts. This should be done in a way that allows the horse a chance to figure out what is expected, and gives him a fair chance to develop the balance and skill necessary to do it easily.

22 Three Thoughts

*A*s dressage books go, this one is not terribly long. Yet, it contains a lot of new information. The idea of "top down" and "bottom up" training.

The concept of five first tier basics. That we can and do ride in mechanical, cognitive, and connected modes. An explanation of how dressage can always be easy, relaxed, and fun for you and your horse. There is a lot more — too much to have at the front of your mind when actually riding. So I'm leaving you with three thoughts I routinely hear myself thinking when working with Horses.

The first is, "The Wise Hunter Goes after One Rabbit at a Time." It is a reminder to me that I need to pick one thing to work on right now. Whatever I decide to work on must be absolutely clear to me, a singular task for the horse to perform, and immediate.

The next is, "Keep Getting a Little Bit Better — Pretty Soon You'll Be Pretty Good." This goes to the core of cognitive training. It means I'm never trying to make my horse be "good" right now. I'm always trying to make him a little bit better. When trying to be good now, it's so easy to fall into the trap of forced mechanical riding. When trying to be just a little better, it's easy to stay relaxed and comfortable.

Remember when I only had the horse *go* enough to be able to work on the other first tier basics? I was satisfied with the horse just moving his feet and compromised on everything else. Now, just a few chapters later, I've built up from those first few lessons in basics to the point I'm working on all the movements. That's how it works with horses. Although I start at the very lowest levels and compromise on everything, I'm always making progress in the form of tiny steps forward, while always trying to help my horse to understand, to stay relaxed, and to stay happy.

Deciding when to compromise and when to move on to the next "rabbit" is solely a matter of rider experience, tact, and feel. Getting experience, tact, and feel involves making mistakes. That's fine. If you're trying something and it's making matters worse rather than better, accept that, learn what you can from it, and move to something else.

Much more important than moving on at exactly the right time, or picking exactly the right exercise, or always riding just the right way, is having exactly the right attitude. This brings me to my third thought, "Attitude Trumps Technique."

Getting this is the easiest thing to do and it makes everything else easy too. Just decide that you're not in any hurry. That you're willing to learn from everything you try — the things that your horse responds well to, and the things that don't help at all. Decide that if your horse isn't doing what you want, it's because he doesn't understand, not because he doesn't want to. With this attitude and the ability to trace all training issues to the five first tier basics, you should do fine.

Maybe there is one more thing - something I don't think of often enough. I used to show up for clinics with some pretty funny looking off the track thoroughbreds like the one I mentioned in the first chapter. Whenever I showed up with a new one, a particular trainer I was especially lucky to learn from would look at him ruefully and say, "Well, he's not going to the Olympics, but you can learn a little dressage and have some fun with him."

That's was a pretty good sentiment and a good thought to end a book with. So, I hope I've helped you to learn a little about dressage, and have some fun with your horse.

Index

A

above the bit, 13, 106

accepting, 16-17, 31, 38

accepting hand, 16, 38

advanced horses, 2, 129

advanced movements, 17, 31, 140

against the aids, 5

aid combination, 32-33

aids, 1-2, 4-6, 12-16, 18-22, 25-27, 31-35, 51, 53-57, 60-61, 63-64, 67, 69-72, 74, 80-85, 89, 93-94, 104, 106-110, 115, 123-124, 126-132, 136-137, 139-140, 145, 152

allowed to perform, 8-9

almost stop, 87, 129

B

balance, 13, 25-27, 34, 47, 60, 63, 68, 106, 108-110, 121-122, 127, 129, 132-133, 135-136, 140, 148, 152-154

basic concepts, 33

basics, 6, 16, 21-22, 26-27, 29, 31-36, 38, 54, 56-57, 61-62, 68, 101, 103, 114, 125, 136, 140, 142, 144, 152, 155-157

behind the aids, 5

belly button, 71, 82-83, 110

bend, 1-2, 13, 19-21, 25, 37-38, 44-45, 48, 53, 69-73, 75, 78-81, 86, 91-92, 106-109, 111, 113, 118-119, 127-133, 139-141, 143-144, 147-151, 153

Big cognitive, 19, 34, 71, 136-137

bolting, 56

bottom up process, 5-6

bottom up, cognitive process, 2

bucking, 56

C

calm, relaxed, and happy, 18, 152

canter, 3, 32, 57, 84, 86, 124, 136, 142, 145, 147-151, 153-154

canter departure, 32

Catch-22, 5, 56, 81

Change of weight, 127

Change through the circle, 125-133, 141-142, 147, 151

P

perform, 6, 8-9, 12-13, 17, 39, 59, 86, 119, 140, 146, 149, 155

performance, 16, 18, 56, 131

physically control, 16

piaffe and passage, 2

pirouettes, 32, 81, 84, 86

poll, 38, 42-43, 46-47, 54, 59, 70, 77, 79, 92-93, 153

poll angle, 46

preparation, 5, 59, 121, 145-147, 149, 154

progress, 6, 27, 35, 38, 57, 73, 82, 104, 156

pulling, 2, 4, 17, 19-20, 37, 43-44, 54, 56, 60, 71, 89, 91, 93, 95, 104, 133, 152

push, 1-2, 20, 37, 50, 54-55, 64, 122

R

reaching into the contact, 92, 111

refined aids, 1, 137

refusing, 56

rein, 19, 21-22, 34, 37, 40-44, 48-49, 53, 61, 63, 65, 71-72, 75, 81, 83, 87, 89, 91, 93-95, 104, 107-108, 129, 135-137

Rein back, 49, 135-137

rein contact, 37, 53, 107

rein length, 41

relaxed muscles, 91

Release of bend, 127, 129

Release of the aids, 67, 71, 74, 83-85, 106, 128-129

resisting, 5

reward, 18, 21-22, 35-36, 39, 43, 49, 56, 61, 72, 82-83, 87, 109, 128, 137, 146

run out, 106, 108

S

school masters, 2, 6, 18

schooling turn, 81, 126, 140-141, 144

seat, 4, 15-16, 31-32, 34, 55-56, 61, 63-64, 93, 121-122, 136, 144

second nature, 27, 126

shoulder-in, 69-70, 104, 108, 113-115, 142-145, 150

shoulders, 49-50, 65, 81, 84, 89

single action, 24

single ideas, 23-25

single tasks, 18, 23

small circle, 13, 109-110, 117

Soften, 6, 13, 20, 25-26, 31, 35, 38-40, 45, 47, 61, 64, 72, 78, 87, 91-93, 95, 97, 99, 107, 109, 123, 129, 135, 137, 145, 152

solve training problems, 4

speed, 25, 53-54, 56, 108, 149

speed, stride and frame, 25

spur, 20

squeezing, 20, 37, 54-55

stiffening, 38, 136

stiffness and tension, 12

Stop, 3-4, 6, 12-13, 16, 19, 25-26, 31, 35, 49, 54, 56-57, 59-65, 67-68, 71, 74, 83-85, 87, 93, 106, 123-124, 126, 128-129, 135-137, 146, 152

straight, 6, 50, 57, 71, 82-84, 86, 106-107, 110, 130-132, 136, 145, 148, 150, 152

straightness, 25, 130-132, 147, 150, 152

stretch, 8, 20, 38, 48, 61, 70, 76, 78, 87, 92-93, 98, 108-109, 127, 141, 145

stretching, 8, 36, 70, 76, 87, 91

submission, 18, 68, 153

supple, 70, 77, 91, 119, 126, 135

T

UVW

3980745R10095

Printed in Great Britain
by Amazon.co.uk, Ltd.,
Marston Gate.